PIG
SIGNALS

LOOK, THINK AND ACT

Jan Hulsen

Kees Scheepens

ROODBONT
PUBLISHERS

VETVICE
Making veterinary knowledge work

Food Safety
Animal Health
Animal Welfare

DR. C.J.M. SCHEEPENS CONSULTANCY B.V

Credits

Authors
Jan Hulsen, Vetvice®
Kees Scheepens, Dr. C.J.M. Scheepens
Consultancy B.V.

Editor
Jan Hulsen, Vetvice®

Final editing
Ton van Schie, Maud van der Woude

English translation
Language Centre Wageningen UR

Final editing English edition
Sue Stewart

Photography
Cover: Axipress
Other photographs: Jan Hulsen
(unless credited otherwise)

Illustrations
Marleen Felius, Dick Rietveld

Design
Erik de Bruin, Dick Rietveld, Varwig Design

Special thanks to:
Henk Altena, Piet Dirven, Martin Fockedey,
Hinnerk Kraneburg, Arno van de Laar, Jan-Paul
Langens, Leo van Leengoed, Arie van Nes,
Roy Nieuwenhuis, John Nijhoff, Mark Roozen,
Marrina Schuttert, Han Smits, Hans Spoolder,
the Raalte Centre for Sustainable and Organic
Pig Farming, *Proefacccomodatie* De Tolakker, the
Sterksel Centre for Innovative Pig Farming,
hundreds of farmers, many vets, farm consul-
tants and feed consultants.

i PUBLISHERS

P.O. Box 4103, NL-7200 BC Zutphen
Telephone: +31 575 54 56 88
Fax: +31 575 54 69 90
E-mail: info@roodbont.nl
Internet: www.roodbont.nl

VETVICE
Making veterinary knowledge work

Moerstraatsebaan 115
NL-4614 PC Bergen op Zoom
Telefoon: : +31 165 30 43 05
Fax: +31 165 30 37 58
E-mail: info@vetvice.nl
Internet: www.vetvice.nl

Food Safety
Animal Health
Animal Welfare

DR. C.J.M. SCHEEPENS CONSULTANCY B.V

Hogevleutweg 5
NL-5681 PD Best
Telephone/Fax: +31 499 31 01 42
E-mail: kscheepens@aol.com
Internet: www.3drie3.nl

Local legislation in certain countries prohibits the
use of certain housing techniques, management
techniques and intervention-techniques. This book
does not want to promote anything which is in
conflict with any kind of legislation in place in a
certain region. However, legislation in different
English-speaking countries might vary in certain
areas of pig husbandry and therefore certain information found in this book might not be applicable
in your country.

ISBN 90-75280-77-7
NUR 940

Table of contents

Focus on the pig

Pig farming is all about pigs. Farm economics and good business practices are important but, if the livestock manager lacks good professional skills, no farm can be successful. This is also evident in practice, where successful farms are characterised by the outstanding care they give their livestock. The livestock managers on these farms all share the same attitude: the pigs always come first. At the same time, a good businessman or woman will ensure that the work is done efficiently, that working conditions are pleasant and that pens, materials and equipment are in good working order.

You raise pigs with your eyes

Some people have the gift of being able to observe and understand pigs, but most people have to learn how to observe and use pig signals. If they decide to become a pig manager, they must be able to observe and understand pigs.

All pig managers are therefore faced with the challenge of acquiring more and more information from their pigs. And we all want to avoid 'farm blindness'; we must find our blind spots and eliminate them. You can do this only if you are open to new things and if you enjoy change. But you must also be critical, seek other people's opinions and keep asking yourself: are things going well or could they be even better?

Dogs look up to us. Cats look down on us.

Pigs treat us as equals.

Winston Churchill

Learn to observe deliberately

Seeing more begins with observing your pigs deliberately, and this is where the book starts. Keep asking yourself questions and actually carry out the improvements needed. Like Sherlock Holmes, livestock managers must also ask questions to arrive at solutions. The three basic questions are:

1. What do I see?
2. Why has this happened?
3. What does this mean?

The final question, "what does this mean," brings you to the moment of truth. What should you do? Carry on as normal, or intervene? This question also helps you choose the best course of action and estimate the cost. Pig Signals® is about looking–thinking–acting.

A practical book

Pig Signals is not just a book to read, it is a book to use. Read it as if you were a pig, sniffing and exploring. Pick a topic, think about a picture puzzle, or simply browse. The book is organised on two levels: the structure of the farm and the structure of the working week. In each case we determine whether the seven basic needs of the pig are met. These are the seven facets of the Pig Signals Diamond: feed-water-light-air-peace & quiet-space-health.

Read *Pig Signals*, put it down, then pick it up again. Leave it on the kitchen table, beside your bed or somewhere else you have the occasional quiet moment to yourself.

Pigs are fun!

Anonymous

CHAPTER 1

See more by seeing better

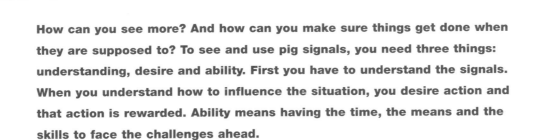

How can you see more? And how can you make sure things get done when they are supposed to? To see and use pig signals, you need three things: understanding, desire and ability. First you have to understand the signals. When you understand how to influence the situation, you desire action and that action is rewarded. Ability means having the time, the means and the skills to face the challenges ahead.

An inspection: here the pig manager does nothing but inspect and take appropriate quick action. Any major interventions are put on a work list.

Looking deliberately

You will see more if you keep asking yourself the three basic questions:

1. **What do I see?**

   Describe what you see completely and objectively so someone who has not seen it knows exactly what you saw.

2. **Why has this happened?**

   Identify the causes of things you see.

3. **What does this mean?**

   Is it good news or bad? Only now should you draw conclusions and intervene if necessary.

Observe deliberately, answer all questions critically and regularly verify the answers; this will stop you becoming 'farm blind'.

To do this, you need to keep an open mind. Never combine inspection with other activities. It is too important.

Bright light means you can see everything, and it ensures pleasant working conditions. The minimum is 200 lux[1].
([1] = 200 lumens per m^2)

An outsider sees things you no longer see yourself. He can help you with questions such as what is good, what is normal, am I thinking along the right lines? Occasionally switch roles between the person asking questions and the person doing the explaining.

From time to time, carry out your inspection round in the opposite direction, in a totally different order. Just look and think.

Focused and open-minded

While observing, focus on your inspection points. These are observations that you know provide specific information. For example, do all of the pigs stand up immediately if you create a disturbance, or do some remain sitting or lying? What does the dung of the sows ready to farrow look like?

Also keep an eye out for Unclassified Notable Observations, or UNOs ('You knows'). Observe with an open mind so that you see things that you weren't looking for. As a result of experience and learning the number of inspection points will grow, but it is still important to observe with an open mind. Observe like an outsider, or like a child.

Quality assurance

A well-conceived approach and good habits produce the most efficient inspections. Clever pen layout, practical walking routes and the right tools make the difference between doing something well and not doing it at all.

Take time for inspections and plan them carefully, never postpone them. Washing down pens is important, but the two inspections of the grower-finishing pigs are more so. Stop working ten minutes before a break to take a quick look in the farrowing pen. Observe all pigs at fixed times. Keep a notebook, use logically-placed notice boards, attention lists and checklists, and make sure experiences are communicated effectively.

Good livestock managers always have their tools handy and make sure the work can be done efficiently. For example, you should be able to inspect and replace nipple drinkers with ease. Farrowing aids should be kept in the farrowing house. Is everything clean, ready and in working order at all times? After all, who wants to break their neck to adjust an intake flap?

Think like a pig

Pigs have their own needs, their own way of doing things and dealing with their environment. This is part of the animal's nature and cannot be changed.

Natural behaviour

In the wild, sows form family groups of two to four sows with their piglets. The habitat of a group is 100 to 500 hectares. The size of the group and its habitat depend on the availability of food. Habitats can overlap. The habitat is centred around a nest where the entire group rests. The pigs defecate in special latrine areas, never in the nest or the foraging area. The group travels through the habitat on trails, where they also defecate and urinate.

Group members harmonise their behaviour: they eat, rest and suckle at the same time. In the wild, sows spend about 70% of the day walking and foraging.

Within both a group and a litter, there is a linear dominance hierarchy. Groups do not mix, new animals are not admitted. Gilts form new groups with each other or with their mothers when they are 7-8 months old. Boars also leave the group at this age. At first they live together with two or three other boars; later they live alone and only come together in a group during the mating season (October-November). They live within the habitats of the sow groups and announce their availability by means of scent tracks. They spread their scent using their urine, saliva and special scent glands in their fore feet.

Knowledge of the natural behaviour and unique needs of pigs helps you to observe, understand and use pig signals.

Pigs have to root. Wild boar eat by moving their snout back and forth and scooping up the food with their lower lip, teeth and tongue. The domestic pig still eats this way, more or less, and also has the need to root.

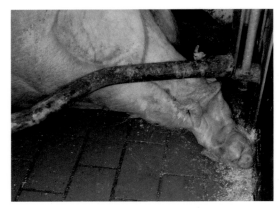

Wild boar also like to eat meat, usually insects and worms. They hunt sometimes, usually for young animals or nests of eggs. On occasion they are lucky enough to find a dead animal. The type of meat does not matter. For this sow, her dead piglet is probably just food.

Hear, see, smell, talk

People see and hear well, but have a poor sense of smell. Vision is less important for the pig, but its senses of smell and hearing are crucial. Pigs talk with other pigs: literally by means of sounds, but also using scent.

Talking

Both domestic and wild pigs produce a variety of grunts, growls and screams that give a clear signal. They can also grind their teeth and smack their lips.

Do you recognise these sounds?

- The stress call: a piercing scream, for example while fighting at the feed trough.
- The alarm sounds made by grower-finishing pigs when startled (a brief "ooh, ooh, ooh").
- Boar sounds such as lip smacking, grunting and the low-pitched, drawn-out grunt.
- The satisfaction call of grower-finishing pigs ("woh-woh-woh").

Many sows with piglets give a warning call if you step into their pen.

Getting acquainted

1. These pigs are raising their snouts quickly and sniffing the air. Their eyes and ears are directed towards the visitor.
2. Pigs are looking, listening and sniffing in the direction of the visitor.
3. The animals are curious and active.

Tasting by rooting and biting is the second step in getting acquainted. A pig will eat almost anything that is edible. Not for nothing is the wild boar known as the "dustman of the wood." Wild boar live mostly on plants, a diet to which their gastrointestinal system and teeth are ideally adapted.

Observing and thinking

The art is to see as many important things as you can in the shortest possible time. Structured observation and structured thinking can help you do this.

When you inspect animals, you get three types of information:

1. **Insight into the situation.** You ask: How are my pigs doing? Do I have their health, well-being and performance under control?
2. **Feedback.** You ask: What were the results of treatments or the causes of anomalies? Was the treatment successful? How did this anomaly occur?
3. **A look ahead.** Based on your observations, you ask: Should I change something now to improve the situation in future?

Look back

You learn by looking back. By determining what caused problems today, you prevent problems tomorrow. But look at your good results as well: what did I do right that caused these pigs to grow so well? Management printouts and slaughter data provide essential information to help you get a complete picture.

Look ahead

The pork production process – from insemination to weaning and from piglet to slaughter – involves a sequence of events. What happens today affects things far into the future. The process also involves a continuous flow of pigs, from one pen to another. Good pig management therefore means constant preparation and always thinking ahead.

Look from large to small (and back)

Observe from large to small. Do not focus immediately on that one pale piglet or that pig that is failing to thrive, but observe the general environment first, then the herd, then the smaller groups in a herd and finally the individual pig. After this, zoom back out from the pig to the big picture.

Why are some sows eating poorly? Is the pen too hot? Is something wrong with the feed or the water?

Look at the big picture: some sows in the compartment did not eat all their feed. Several litters are agitated.

Focus on the details: check the health of the sows. Are they alert, do they have a fever? Are the teats hot or swollen? Are there any other disease symptoms?

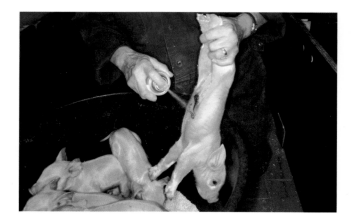

Standard disinfection procedure ensures that the navel heals quickly and limits the risk of bacteria entering the wound and causing infection. This gives piglets more resistance right from the start.

Pressure of infection and resistance

The health of livestock depends on their resistance to disease and the pressure of infection. Health, well-being and a good feed and water intake are the cornerstones of resistance. Healthy, well-fed and cared-for pigs have more resistance than that provided by vaccination alone. It is important that animals do not lose their built-up resistance. In the case of pigs, the resistance of the skin and mucous membranes is important. Wounds and damage to the surface (mucous membranes) of airways and intestines are an entryway for pathogens. Until they are weaned, piglets are almost totally dependent on the resistance they receive from the colostrum and milk. Pressure of infection = the number of pathogens x their pathogenicity (capability to cause disease).

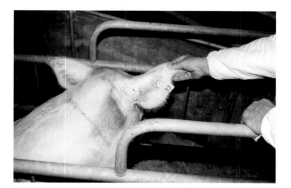

Skin haemorrhaging caused by classical swine fever, a highly pathogenic virus. It only takes a few virus particles to make a pig sick.

Stress
● Stress happens when pigs are exposed to conditions they don't like but are unable to change. Fights, changes and draughty surroundings lead to stress.
● Stress lowers resistance. Stressed pigs tend to rest, eat and drink less; their immune systems are disrupted.

Photo: Mark Roozen

This pig may have a viral infection. Infection with many mild pathogens can lead to 'syndrome diseases' such as PMWS/PDNS[2] and respiratory diseases including PRDC[3]. Viruses such as PRRS[4] and PCV[5] and bacteria such as App[6], mycoplasma, staphylococci and streptococci are present in large quantities on many farms.

[2] *Post-weaning Multisystemic Wasting Syndrome/Porcine Dermatitis and Nephropathy Syndrome*
[3] *Porcine Respiratory Disease Complex*
[4] *Porcine Reproductive and Respiratory Syndrome*
[5] *Porcine Circovirus*
[6] *Actinobacillus Pleuropneumonia*

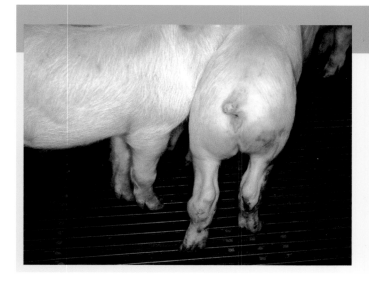

Picture puzzle
What does this picture tell you?

1. One piglet has a swollen hock joint, another has a swollen knee. Both have joint inflammations.
2. Bacteria entered the bloodstream through wounds and settled in the joints. Inflammations lower immunity and bacteria increase the risk of new infections. These animals have more difficulty at times of risk, such as weaning and moving to new pens/mixing with new pigs.
3. Identify risk moments and risk locations before bacteria can enter the body. Eliminate these risks wherever possible.

The Pig Signals Diamond

Lists and memory aids help you to make efficient inspections. Keep thinking clearly during this process. For example, make sure you keep the ends and the means separate. An end is providing for the piglets' need to play, a means is hanging a chain in the pen. The Pig Signals Diamond summarises the basic needs of the pig: these are the ends. For each farm, animal group and time period, these needs can be satisfied in different ways: these are the means. Always keep this diamond in mind when making inspections.

Feed
Every pig can eat sufficient amounts of good quality feed.

Water
Every pig can drink sufficient amounts of good quality water.

Light
The amount and duration of light support a normal biorhythm.

Light
Every pig can breathe unlimited fresh air.

Peace & quiet
Every pig has a resting place with a comfortable microclimate.

Space
Every pig has space for its behavioural needs such as resting, foraging, playing, defecation and urination.

Health
Every pig is free of infectious diseases, other disorders and injuries.

The Pig Signals Diamond in practice

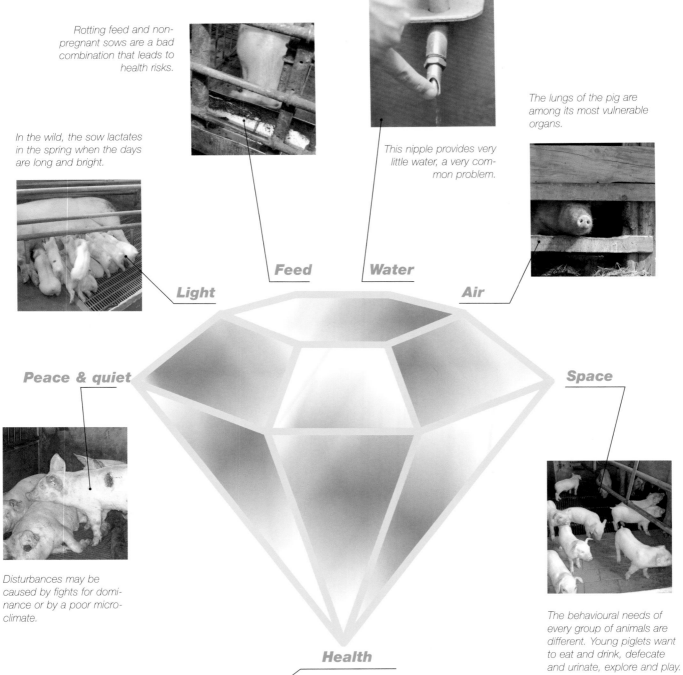

Rotting feed and non-pregnant sows are a bad combination that leads to health risks.

In the wild, the sow lactates in the spring when the days are long and bright.

This nipple provides very little water, a very common problem.

The lungs of the pig are among its most vulnerable organs.

Light

Feed

Water

Air

Peace & quiet

Space

Disturbances may be caused by fights for dominance or by a poor micro-climate.

The behavioural needs of every group of animals are different. Young piglets want to eat and drink, defecate and urinate, explore and play.

Health

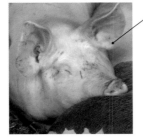

Infections and diseases require constant alertness, hygiene, treatment and prevention.

Information moments

Every moment provides its own information. For example, when the pigs are completely at rest you can evaluate their lying behaviour, which also tells you something about the climate. If they are startled, you can immediately see which animals are slower to respond.

Risks

Besides success factors (see the Pig Signals Diamond), also pay attention to risks and Unclassified Notable Observations (UNO, 'You know'). Risks can be evaluated separately, such as the risk of E. coli diarrhoea or of abortion. Risks can be classified according to risk locations, risk moments and risk groups.

In risk situations, ask yourself:

1. What are the risks?
2. How can I minimise these risks?
3. How can I identify risks early and how do I intervene?

Risk locations

Any location where a pig could be exposed to disease or distress.

In this pen it is difficult to maintain a good microclimate for piglets. There are cold draughts from the manure pit. The rubber mat serves as a warm lying place, and the straw prevents cannibalism.

Pasture-raised pigs have contact with other animals and live in a pathogen-rich environment. These pigs run an increased risk of infections such as gastro-intestinal worms and tapeworms from pig manure and contaminated soil, toxoplasmosis from cat faeces and erysipelas caused by a soil bacterium.

Risk groups

Groups (batches) of pigs that run an increased risk of certain problems. Risk groups are therefore a good control; if they are doing well, the likelihood is that all the pigs are doing well.

Examples of risk groups:

- sows recently introduced to the group
- piglets with a low birth weight (<1 kg)
- farrowing sows with poor mobility
- overly thin or obese sows
- pigs with wounds

Gilts are a risk group in group housing situations. This is especially true when they are moved to the farrowing unit, where they experience many changes and come into contact with many new things. In the meantime they must eat and drink optimally.

Piglets that eat little feed in the farrowing pen take longest after weaning to adapt to solid feed. Because they have drunk a great deal of milk, they are often the best piglets, but the long fasting period leads to post-weaning diarrhoea or bowel oedema.

Risk moments

Times when there is a high probability of pigs having problems or when things can go wrong. Times like these require increased alertness.

Examples of risk moments:
- weaning
- a new stockman
- a change of feed
- farrowing and birth

An intervention is an especially risky moment. This causes stress and often injures the animal. Working in a calm, organised and very careful fashion minimises any harm to the pig. Be very critical and always perform routine interventions correctly.

Moving pigs is a risk moment because they become stressed and are then obliged to seek rest, food and water again. Mixing with other pigs increases these risks and spreads infection.

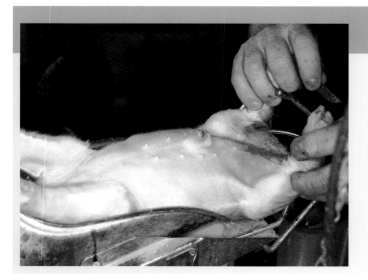

Picture Puzzle
What does this picture tell you

1. A pig is being castrated in a holder. Blood covers much of its hindquarters. Its navel is red and swollen.
2. Its navel is infected. Possible causes: the navel was not disinfected, a rough or dirty floor, or poor resistance. The wound and surrounding area have not been cleaned.
3. The holding device allows you to work carefully. Blood and crusted blood increase the risk of the castration wound becoming infected. The infected navel lowers the piglet's resistance. Treat the navel infection and clean and disinfect the castration wound. Review navel care and castration procedure.

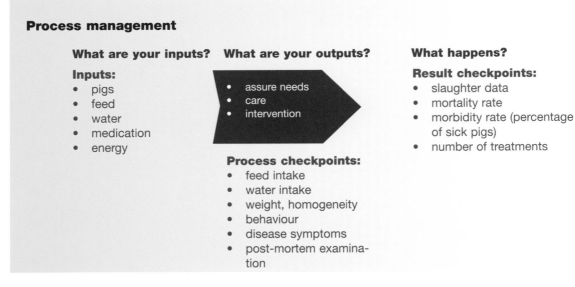

Process management

What are your inputs?

Inputs:
- pigs
- feed
- water
- medication
- energy

What are your outputs?
- assure needs
- care
- intervention

Process checkpoints:
- feed intake
- water intake
- weight, homogeneity
- behaviour
- disease symptoms
- post-mortem examination

What happens?

Result checkpoints:
- slaughter data
- mortality rate
- morbidity rate (percentage of sick pigs)
- number of treatments

The process checkpoints and result checkpoints tell you if you need to do things differently or include other things in the process: different feed, different pigs, more time, etc.

Healthy or sick?

The clinical examination focuses on two questions. What do I see? Why has this happened? The interim question – Is this right? – directs the examination and tells you if it has been sufficient. The treatment and prevention plan emerge from the third question: What does it mean? And this can lead in turn to more questions.

Infection = contamination with pathogens

Observing at herd level

Besides observing individual pigs, the livestock manager should also look at the big picture: herds and processes. Diagrams and drawings help you understand and work with the big picture.

Uniformity and averages play an important role in herd inspection. What is the average growth? Do all pigs achieve this growth or do many deviate from the norm? Uniformity makes inspection easier, because every pig that stands out from a uniform group is a signal.

Disease symptoms and behaviour tell you something about the animals' degree of health and comfort.

If symptoms are observed, the seriousness of the symptom and the number of animals affected are important. When evaluating behaviour, individual pigs require attention. Chronic biting behaviour can begin with a single agitated pig.

Step-by-step plan for clinical examination

1. History

What is the history of the animals (feed, care and housing)?

Differential diagnosis list

Sometimes it is possible to identify the cause of an illness beyond all doubt; however, there are usually several possible causes. As a result, a vet always works with a list of differential diagnoses, with the most probable one at the top.

2. General impression

Observe the pig and other members of the herd. Use the Pig Signals Diamond as a guide.

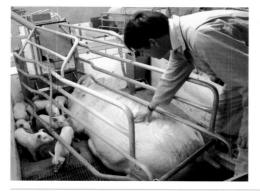

3. General examination

Always carry out the basic checks.
- *Feed intake and dung production.*
- *Respiration: rate and rhythm of breathing, including flank movements*
- *Temperature: temperature of other pigs in the herd and unit.*
- *Skin-hair-hooves: look at colour, damage and abnormal growth.*
- *Teats and vulva: look at colour, swelling, injury, discharge.*
- *Mucous membranes: look at colour and swelling.*
- *Look at body posture and movements.*
- *Anything unusual.*

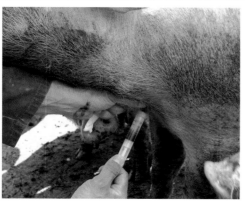

4. Further examination

The examination question (what do I want to know?) determines the type of examination and selection of specimens. Allow the vet to select the right pigs carefully and supply sufficient specimens. Further examination can include:
- *Lab work (blood tests or dung samples).*
- *Post-mortem examination of animals or slaughterhouse material.*
- *Climate evaluation. Evaluate the information obtained. Are you sure about the diagnosis and approach? Or is further investigation required?*
- *Other possibilities.*

Anatomy

If you understand how a pig is put together, many pig signals become logical and understandable. In order to tell someone else exactly what you have observed, you also have to know the correct names of the parts. And so does the other person.

1	Lower lip	19	Hock joint
2	Snout	20	Fetlock
3	Bridge of nose	21	Dewclaw
4	Ear base	22	Coronary band
5	Neck	23	Heel
6	Shoulder	24	Hoof
7	Withers	25	Groin
8	Ribs	26	Teats
9	Back	27	Belly
10	Loin	28	Chest
11	Rear flank	29	Elbow
12	Rump	30	Sternum
13	Hook bone	31	Point of shoulder
14	Anus	32	Knee
15	Vulva	33	Pastern
16	Pin bone	34	Interdigital space
17	Ham	35	Throat
18	Hock	36	Cheek

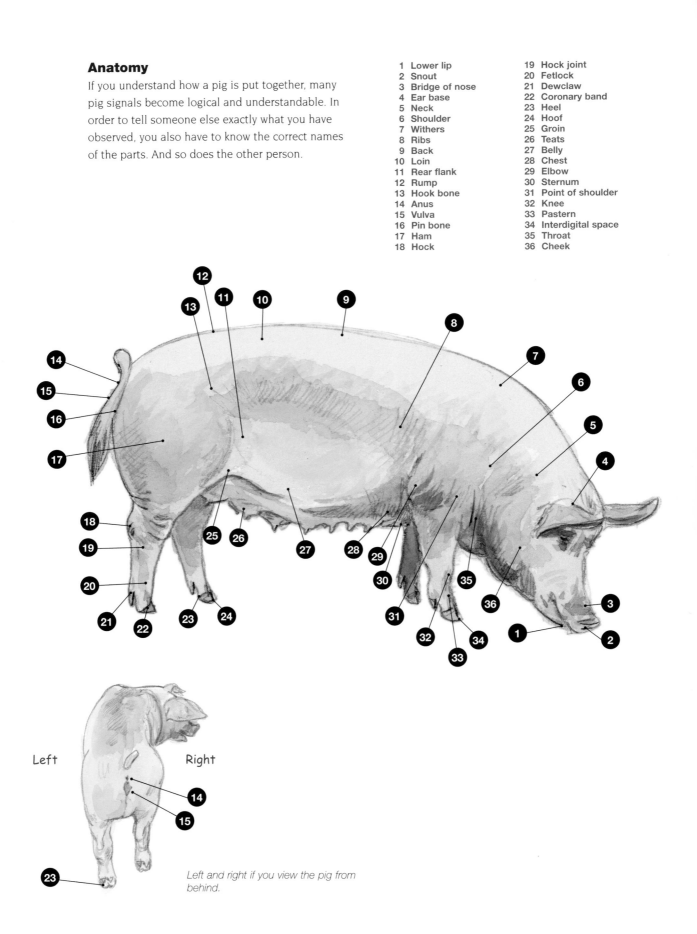

Left   Right

Left and right if you view the pig from behind.

1	Nose bone	13	Pin bone	27	Sternum
2	Upper jaw	14	Femur	28	Elbow
3	Skull	15	Tibia	29	Knee
4	Cervical vertebrae (7 vertebrae)	16	Fibula	30	Ulna
5	Shoulder blade	17	Hock	31	Radius
6	Thoracic vertebrae	18	Hock joint	32	Elbow joint
	(13 to 16 vertebrae)	19	Metatarsal bones	33	Humerus
7	Lumbar vertebrae	20	Pasterns; cannon bones	34	Shoulder joint
	(5 to 8 vertebrae)	21	Knuckle bones	35	Mandibular joint
8	Hook bone	22	Short pastern bones	36	Lower jaw
9	Sacrum	23	Phalanges	37	Molars
10	Hip bone	24	Stifle joint	38	Canine (tusk)
11	Coccygeal vertebrae	25	Ribs	39	Incisors
12	Hip joint	26	Rib cartilages		

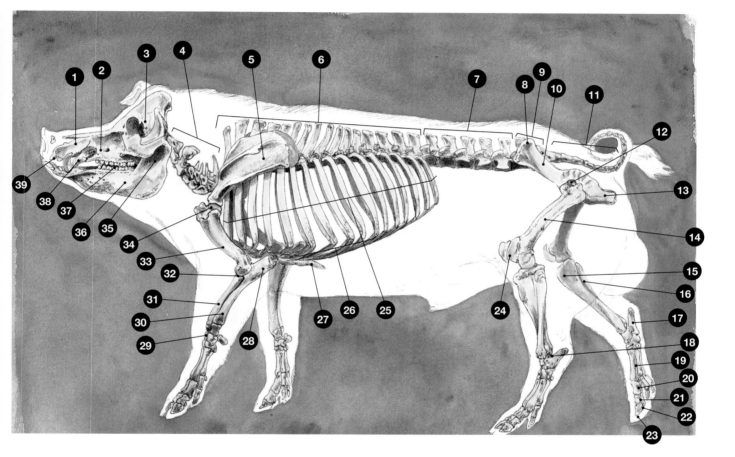

Position of the organs in the chest and abdominal cavities

1 Lung
2 Heart
3 Diaphragm
4 Liver
5 Small intestine
6 Large intestine

Not shown:
Stomach
Spleen (elongated, purple/red)
Kidneys (towards the back)

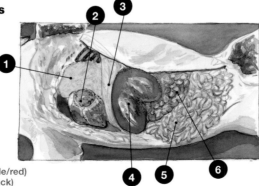

Abdominal and thoracic membranes

The chest cavity has an airtight separation (diaphragm) from the abdominal cavity. The chest cavity contains the lungs and heart, which are relatively small in pigs. All organs are contained within the abdominal and thoracic membranes; these also cover the abdominal and the chest walls. The membranes contain some moisture, which ensures that the organs and walls can move easily against each other.

CHAPTER 2

Pregnant sows and gilts

These sows are displaying natural use of their habitat. A nest to rest in, a toilet or latrine area and an area in which to eat and explore.

If all goes well, little of any note happens during the three months, three weeks and three days of normal pig gestation. Pregnant animals engage in daily routines such as eating, drinking and defecating. They may receive the odd a vaccination. Due to these routines, there is a risk that the sows will be given too little attention, even though pregnancy is a very important time.

Purpose of the farrowing house

At the end of her pregnancy, the sow is ready to farrow and raise a healthy litter. This means that her condition, feed intake and health are all geared specifically to the gestation period. Her aim is to produce the largest possible number of vital piglets. By the daily monitoring of housing and care, you assure your sows' health, well-being and performance.

In nature

Wild boar sows are pregnant for around 119 days and usually farrow once a year. Domestic pigs are pregnant for 114 days and farrow more than 2.2 times a year. Domestic sows are therefore pregnant for more than 250 days a year.

Animals that need attention and indicator animals

Risk groups allow you to identify the limits of care and housing. They are the first to show that specific matters require improvement. If the risk groups are doing well, then the other pigs will do well. Gilts are a risk group for example, as are sows that have difficulty standing, lying down, remaining in a lying position and walking.

Gilts

Gilts are given the worst places to lie and are regularly put in their place by older sows. A gilt gets less rest, even though she has a great deal to learn and is busy meeting the demands of her developing body. The greatest risks are hoof problems and poor physical development. And after this, another difficult time awaits her in the farrowing house.

Agitation

Even for gilts, stress must be kept to a minimum, especially during vulnerable periods such as after insemination and around farrowing. At these times, shield the animals from contact with the unfamiliar and the unexpected if possible. Even better, introduce the gilts to group housing and the farrowing pen in advance. A separate gilt group also creates a safer environment.

Introduce gilts (and older sows) to the larger group in small groups. Since the animals often know each other, this will enable them to form a subgroup. The larger the space and the number of pigs in the group, the easier it is to introduce new pigs. There is always a safe hiding place or a piece of neutral territory.

Look-think-act
How do you deal with poor mobility?

This sow is favouring her left hind foot and arching her back to distribute weight over the other three legs. She has an abscess on her right front knee, is lame and probably has been for a while.

The animal is still eating well, as demonstrated by her exploring behaviour, full belly, condition and her colour and sheen. But as she gains weight, she runs a high risk of developing pressure sores and becoming emaciated.

This sow belongs in a hospital pen on straw.

Light · Feed · Water · Air
Peace & quiet · Space
Health

Feed pigs with your eyes

Early pregnancy

A pregnant sow must grow into ideal condition, after which her back fat must remain constant. During the first half of gestation, she uses the feed to improve her own condition. After that it all goes to nourish the piglets. The condition of the sow is the most important focus for feeding. And there is a second focus: piglet uniformity. Differences in birth weight are closely related to the nutrition of the piglet during the first month of pregnancy. The quality of the foetal membrane and navel cord, and the supply of nutrients from the uterus, play a role in this respect.

Late pregnancy

The health of the sows and the average birth weight of the piglets are your aims and benchmarks during the final phase (last third) of pregnancy. During the last three weeks, the piglets nearly double in weight.

Ensure that the sow continues to eat and drink sufficiently; her dung should also remain soft. The composition of the feed can be checked in this way. Danger signs are excessive firmness of their udder before farrowing and, after farrowing, problems with poor lactation, poor eating and large numbers of sick sows.

Monitoring feed intake
Are they getting enough?

Most feeding systems measure portions in litres, but the weight of the mixed feed varies. You should know the weight per litre of every shipment of feed to ensure that the animals get the right amount. Measure this by weighing a portion, or 10 litres of feed.

Are they all eating?

A note on the attention list, a feed trough that is not empty, a belly that is not full. These are the most important signals that a sow is not eating enough.

What are they eating?

The dung gives an insight into the composition of the feed the sow is eating. This sow is eating a lot of straw. Performance, health and appetite also provide information. Feed composition means not only the amounts of nutrients, but also contaminants and spoilage.

Activity peaks

Sows naturally eat at the same time and rest at the same time: in the morning. They usually drink after eating, when they can easily take six litres or more. Wild sows spend about 60% of their time rooting and eating when they are pregnant. These are diurnal animals, but easily switch to a night rhythm.

Depending on the feeding system, pregnant sows eat simultaneously or in turns. Every feeding leads to an activity peak. The same happens when a new feeding period begins at the feeding station.

If sows eat simultaneously, they also drink simultaneously. The drinking water system must provide enough for all sows to drink adequately (1 l/min). If a sow has to wait too long, she may drink less water than is desirable.

Risk moment

The transition from gestation feed to lactation feed in the farrowing house is a time of risk . During this period, the intestines must remain filled. Make sure that the crude fibre source in the feed stays the same and that the sows eat and drink well.

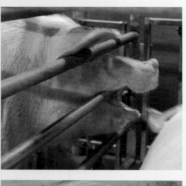

Satiation

Pigs begin sham chewing and bar biting if they are not satiated. Provide a few hundred grams of roughage, such as straw or pulp. Ensure that the pigs are satiated.

Pigs are satiated by chewing (straw), the sensation of fullness in their stomach and intestines (straw, pulp) and the digestive products of fibres (especially fatty acids).

Look-think-act
What does the white spot mean?

The white area can be caused by either pus or urine crystals. Pus indicates a bladder infection. Blood in the urine is also a symptom of bladder or kidney infection. Urine crystals are caused by bladder infection and by certain feeding errors or metabolic diseases.

The main cause of bladder infection is a shortage of drinking water. Other causes are infections after farrowing and insemination.

Light Feed Water Air
Peace & quiet Space
Health

The environment

A pig divides its environment into usage areas: a resting area, an eating area and a defecating area. The animal recognises these areas primarily by their smells. The usage areas are separated by paths. Pigs usually urinate where they defecate, but sometimes on the paths as well.

Resting area

The resting area provides a comfortable lying area that is soft and with a pleasant climate, not too hot, not too cold, no draughts, no disturbances by other pigs. In nature, the rest areas are hidden deep in the undergrowth.

Defecating area

The defecating area allows a pig to defecate without being disturbed. The smell of manure prompts the pigs to defecate. Defecation areas must be at least five and no more than fifteen meters from the feeding areas.

Feeding area

At the feeding area, the pig can eat undisturbed. It is important that the animals cannot monopolise the food or take food from each other.

Paths

The aisles are recognisable and can serve as paths. This means that there is sufficient space between lying, eating and defecating areas. It also means that the pigs can move about safely: with sufficient grip and without hazards from hard floor components that can damage their hooves.

Heat is a problem for pregnant sows, certainly for those ready to farrow. Their natural cooling response is to take mud baths. Ventilation, insulation, high ceilings and protection from sun help to keep the pen cool. Adequate ventilation also assures dry floors.

These sows have their resting areas against the side walls. The defecation area is in the middle. Sows are lying near or in the defecation area. This indicates that the space is too small for the number of sows.

Lack of space in group housing

A large group of pigs divides itself into smaller groups of about four animals, which then adapt their habitats to each other. If you divide the pens up into small lying areas with clear paths and free areas for defecation, you steer the pigs in the desired direction. For example, one group should not defecate in another's resting area.

Straw bedding

Groups form and specific lying areas develop on straw bedding as well, although at first glance the pigs appear to be lying randomly in the area. The animals have more or less fixed positions, move along fixed routes and have a fixed defecation area. The colours indicate how the pigs experience the spaces: lying areas (blue, green, red areas), walking routes to the defecation areas (arrows), and an area where all pigs display exploring behaviour (lavender).

Slatted floor

This pen design directs the pigs to the desired use. Separate lying areas encourage the forming of groups. By closing off lying areas when the pen is not fully occupied, improper use can be prevented (such as defecation); it is difficult to reverse improper usage if the area is needed again as a lying area. Newcomers may initially be required to stay for a time in the defecation area. As soon as they are accepted, they take a place in a lying area. Pigs choose a defecation area where they can defecate quietly and without disturbance.

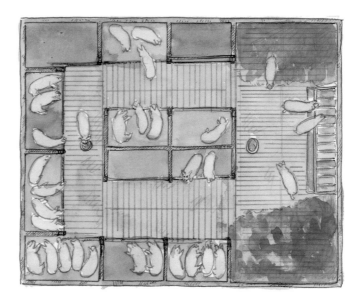

Light Feed Water Air
Peace & quiet Space
Health

Health

Regarding the health of pregnant sows, a small number of diseases and injuries cause most problems. The main diseases affecting this group are parvo, PRRS and influenza. And of course there are threats from more general diseases, such as swine erysipelas, gastrointestinal worms, mange – and in the past – Aujeszky's disease.

Many of these diseases are no longer a problem due to successful control programmes such as vaccination against parvo and erysipelas, and the elimination of Aujeszky's disease. Disorders such as mange, gastrointestinal worms and PRRS must be kept under control by means of continuous prevention and treatment. A brief lapse of attention can lead to serious problems (if these diseases appear on the farm, because both mange and PRRS should be eliminated).

Main issues and side issues
80% of the problems stem from 20% of the possible causes.

A typical example of a sick pig, where you can't immediately tell what is wrong. The clinical pictures of many diseases are very similar, so consult a vet periodically and have lab tests and post-mortems done.

Injuries

Hoof problems are the second group of health risks. They occur if the load is heavier than the hoof can bear, for example if the animal moves abruptly when startled. The floor also plays a role in this respect. A slatted floor does not provide complete support, and the edge of a slat can cause a focused load on the hooves. Wet hooves become soft. They cannot support as much weight and are more easily penetrated by bacteria.

The preferential sites for hoof and coronary band injuries.

This sow may be lame or having difficulty in standing for other reasons. This is an indicator animal. She will be the first to notice if the floor is too slippery.

A pressure sore/abrasion caused by injury from the floor. The hock shows a callus with thickening of the skin.

Good mobility

Because pigs in group housing move about, they develop strong muscles, bones, tendons and joints. Gilts must also be physically strong enough to hold their own in group housing. This requires roomy housing for gilts or a gradual transition via a gilt group.

New additions pen

Keep newly-arrived gilts and boars in a quarantine pen for at least six weeks. Allow any viral diseases to run their course until the animals are no longer contagious. Let them become accustomed to the pathogens on the farm, for example by exposing them to the manure of older sows or a sow destined for culling. The new arrivals may become sick, which means that the design of the quarantine pen must meet stringent requirements.

Loss of embryos

Avoid stress between day 4 and day 30 after insemination. Embryos can die easily in the first three to four weeks, and are then absorbed by the uterus wall. If five or fewer embryos remain, the pregnancy ends and the sow returns to oestrus. Embryos that die after day 50 are no longer reabsorbed. They become mummified or are aborted. Other reasons for abortion besides disease are disturbances caused by fighting at the trough, or rough handling by the stockman. Embryo loss shortly before the farrowing date leads to still-birth.

Lameness in gilts is often related to jumping, startling and escaping. This may occur during oestrus and while fighting.

Parvo virus infection is an important cause of mummified piglets, but they can also be caused by other infections.

Look-think-act
What is happening here?

This low-ranking sow is obliged to lie in the defecation area. She is sham chewing. The small pen provides insufficient lying space, which soon leads to pressure sores. Moisture and urine soak the skin, causing pressure sores. The rough floor exacerbates this process. If a pig is lying in manure, it means she is too hot or lacks space.

Inspections

Inspecting animals is essential if you want to detect problems early. Use checklists and write down the results. This stops you overlooking or forgetting things.

Sow inspections

Signal	Immediate action	Follow-up action
Attention lists automatic feeder/feed intake	Inspect sows needing attention	
Active, alert?	Modify treatment plan	Take temperatures
Stands up easily?	Modify treatment plan	Severity, observe progression
Injuries?	Eliminate cause	Provide treatment
Too hot/too cold, behaviour		Eliminate cause
Soiling		Eliminate cause
Soft dung?	Modify rations	Check water intake
Abortion	Identify cause	Identify sow
Anything unusual?	Eliminate cause	Provide treatment
10% of the sows stand in a group	Remove disturbance, check feeding station	

When inspecting individual sows, it is also useful to write down your observations. First of all, it ensures that others can carry on your work and, second, it helps in identifying exactly how specific disorders and treatments occurred.

When evaluating herd signals, pay attention to smaller groups within the larger herd. If you see a number of pigs breathing rapidly, for example, this may be a signal to turn on the ventilation fan for more cooling.

Herd	Which sows?	Cause?
All animals are quiet.		
Are they all lying in the rest area?		
Are they all lying on their sides?		
Do they show warmth-seeking behaviour?		
Do they show cool-seeking behaviour?		
Is the herd uniform in terms of:	**average**	**deviation**
· condition/back fat		
· development		
· mobility		
· soiling		
· colour and sheen		
· injuries		
Which animals stand out?		
Can every pig walk around comfortably?		
Anything unusual?		

A risk location. Check the water pressure at the most distant points of the water system, immediately after feeding when all sows are drinking. This is when all sows should be able to drink as much as they want.

In the farrowing house it will become clear if the pregnant sow has been properly fed and cared for. Check this and use the findings to improve the situation.

In the farrowing house	
Varying litters	
Dead or mummified piglets	
Sow farrows well	
All piglets have full bellies	
Sow eats well, udder is full and not hot, no fever (<39.5°C)	

CHAPTER 3

In the farrowing house

The farrowing period is a crucial period filled with risks for sows and piglets. They must be strong and healthy, and stay that way, if they are to get through this period successfully. This places high demands on housing, nutrition and care.

The farrowing period demands top performance from sow, piglet and stockman.

Sow and piglets share the space in the farrowing pen, but the needs of the sow and those of the piglets are not always identical. This results in difficult situations. For example, newborn piglets want their lying area at body temperature, but this is much too hot for the sow, who does not want it any warmer than 21°C. Moreover, besides being a source of food for the piglets, the sow is also a hazard; she may crush or savage the piglets. In the farrowing pen, the sow experiences many changes, and lactation places heavy demands on her. After four weeks, the piglets should be able to look after themselves and have laid the foundations for a healthy life.

There is a lot to do in the farrowing house. Pay extra attention to organisation, walking routes and ergonomics in the design of the farrowing house. The lengthwise positioning of this pen makes it easy to carry out inspections and take action.

Aggression

Aggression is the first response of the farrowing sow to intruders and stress factors. Stress can make the sow become aggressive towards her own piglets. This aggression is especially common in sows farrowing for the first time. The pain of contractions, dilation and birth often causes this redirected behaviour. After farrowing, maternal instinct usually overcomes her aggression and the sow accepts the piglets. Breeding lines differ greatly in their maternal qualities.

In the wild
A few days before farrowing, the sow separates herself from the group. She makes a nest where she can farrow and spend the first few days with her piglets in complete isolation. This nest is located 100 metres or more from the common nest. Nest building stimulates later maternal care. The sow responds aggressively to other sows – and people – by chasing them away. She is on special alert for the natural enemies of her piglets such as foxes.

Three key words

Three key words apply to your work in the farrowing house.
1. **Always** Every piglet and every sow all the time.
2. **Meticulous** Piglets and sows are vulnerable. 'Almost good enough' is never good enough.
3. **Smart** Work easily, inexpensively, do it right the first time.

Three key individuals

There are three key individuals in the farrowing house.
1. **The sow** must be comfortable when lying, suckling, eating and drinking.
2. **The piglet** must be comfortable when eating, drinking, lying and playing.
3. **The stockman** must be able to work comfortably.

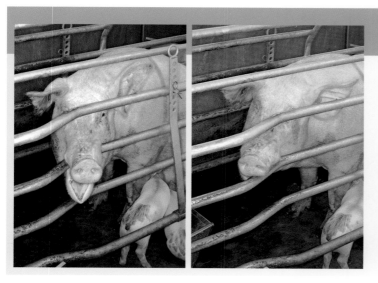

Look-think-act
What do you see?

While you are observing this sow, you take a step closer and she bites the rail. You take a step back, and she stops. This is redirected behaviour: the sow wants to chase you (the intruder) away when you enter her nesting area. But she cannot attack you so focuses her aggression on the rail.

Be prepared

Is the sow ready to farrow and suckle?

Before and after farrowing, sows must continue to eat and drink properly. This means easily accessible feed of the right composition and plenty of water. The sow must be able to stand up and remain standing easily and be able to eat and drink undisturbed. More than two feeds per day ensure a higher feed intake.

Changes, transitions and stress reduce feed intake. Avoid changes, or handle them very carefully. Gilts are even more vulnerable; for them everything is new.

The preparturient sow in the farrowing house runs a nutritional risk. She must continue to eat and drink well and produce soft dung. This reduces the risk of poor farrowing outcomes and insufficient milk after farrowing (PHS or MMA).

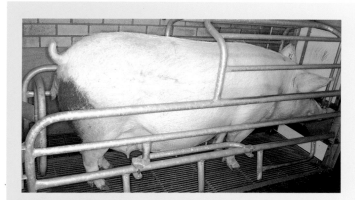

Stands easily

This is a heavy sow who has trouble standing up; as a result she has trodden on her rear teats. Animals must be strong to stand up with so much weight, the rail must not be in the way and the hooves must have a good grip on the floor. Fat sows eat less and have more difficulty standing.

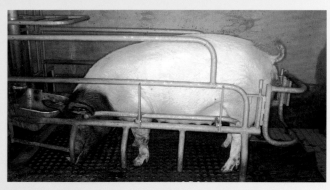

A rubber mat provides good grip so the sow can stand up easily. The holes provide drainage. The rubber mat was installed immediately after this sow was found to have problems. The mat will remain in place until weaning, ensuring that the sow eats and drinks optimally. She will lose the minimum amount of weight and will lie comfortably.

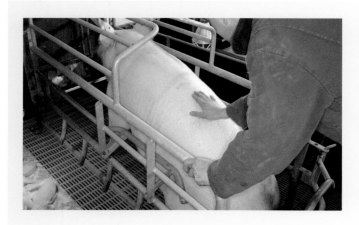

Checking how the sow stands up

Watching quietly while a sow stands up usually tells you if she does this with sufficient ease and where the problem lies. If the sow lingers when roused and gives a piercing high-pitched stress call, this is a sign that she has trouble standing up.

Dung evaluation for sows

Soft manure: *glistening, well-formed mass. Yields to the touch; broken surface is glossy*

Dung too hard: *rounded pellets with a dull gloss. Force is needed to break them. The fracture surface has a dull gloss. Cause: intestinal transit is too slow due to unsuitable feed and/or insufficient water intake.*

Imminent birth

The sow is initially agitated and displays nest-building behaviour. About six hours before the birth, colostrum can be expressed from the teat and the sow becomes agitated.

Ready to drink as much colostrum as possible?

Are the pen and sow ready so that every piglet can quickly and easily get to the teat and drink colostrum? The greatest danger is chilling: piglets that are too cold behave as if they were drunk. Provide a clean space behind the sow that is not too cold, not too slippery and does not cause any injuries.

Ready to help?

If all your tools are clean and within reach, you will be able to use them when you need them. Make sure you are nearby and make regular checks when a sow is farrowing.

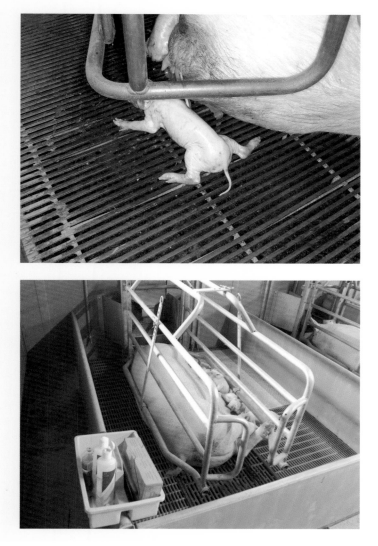

The first day

Strong piglets who are able to find the teats and drink plenty of colostrum, which is what the first day is all about. Each piglet must find its own way, navigating by the scent of the udder, the direction of hair growth and the sounds made by the sow.

Two piglets are having difficulty finding the teats. The yellow feed trough serves no function and does not belong there. It just gets in their way. Work calmly and quietly when you place the piglets near the udder. Sows are calm if the stockman is calm.

Farrowing

If all goes well, piglets drink fifteen meals of 15 ml of colostrum each in the first twelve hours. Colostrum contains the fuel which keeps the piglets warm.

During the first few hours, the sow provides milk constantly. Later on, her piglets suckle periodi-cally with breaks of about one hour. Farrowing usually takes fifteen minutes per piglet. If it takes longer, this indicates that the sow is not in optimal health or that the piglet is positioned incorrectly.

Fostering (more piglets than teats)

Fostering should always benefit the piglet. Bear in mind that new battles for dominance reduce colostrum intake and resistance. Any wounds that occur are entryways for infection. Fostering is useful only if a piglet is not able to can drink sufficient milk from the sow. Do this on the second day and make sure that the piglet drinks plenty of colostrum.

Uniform litters make it easier to conduct inspections. Piglets that have problems are more obvious, but all piglets suffer due to vicious fights for dominance. The difference in strength between piglets is minimal, so it takes longer for a winner to emerge. When you foster piglets, you also transfer infections. The older the piglet, the greater the risk.

Colostrum is essential. The newborn piglet does not have any antibodies of its own. It needs energy, partly to keep itself warm. The protein provides nutrients and antibodies.

Nutrients

Energy

Antibodies

Crushing

Due to her body weight, the sow lies down with a flop even when she is being careful. Piglets can easily become trapped under her body. Both the sow and the piglets play a role in this respect. A sow should be able to stand up easily; she needs good mobility and a good grip on the floor. The piglets must have a roomy and comfortable nest. If they do, they are less likely to lie exactly where the sow does (the floor stays warm long after the sow stands up).

Chilled piglets seek warmth and crawl close to the sow. Chilled animals are slow to react, for example to the sow lying down from a sitting position.

Don't wait too long

If more than 45 minutes elapses between piglets or if the last piglet has dried off completely, you should intervene. Know what you are doing. Make sure the vulva and your arms are clean, and use plenty of lubricant.

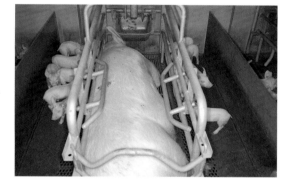

Adequate restraints ensure that the sow lies down more slowly. But too many restraints prevent her from responding to the screams of a trapped piglet. There is also a risk that the sow will not stand up to eat and drink often enough or that she could injure herself. Make sure that the udder is accessible.

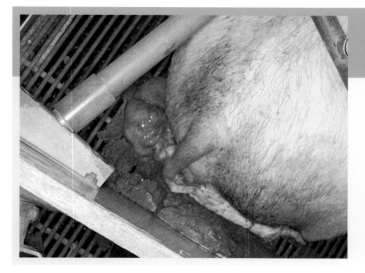

Look-think-act
You are working on a pig farm and you see this. What do you do?

There is no space behind the sow, which causes the piglets to become trapped during farrowing. A cross-bar often helps to keep the sow towards the front of the box. But this box is too short: you must provide more space. Dung contains pathogens and should be cleaned up.

Light — Feed — Water — Air
Peace & quiet — Space
Health

Evaluating feed intake

During an inspection you can see if the sow and piglets have eaten enough today. This page describes the important signals.

Any changes that you observe also provide important information: sows and piglets that behave differently, different sounds, different scents. To observe this, the stockman must remain alert and there must be good communication between the various people working with the pigs.

Sequence of a normal feed

The sow lies on her side and invites the piglets to suckle by making a certain grunting sound. The piglets begin to root and suckle, which stimulates the flow of milk. Often a piglet will approach the sow's head and ask for milk by grunting.

The sow gives milk freely for about 30 seconds, which she indicates with a periodic, deep 'groink-groink-groink' sound. When the sow stops giving milk, she makes a different sound. The piglets continue to massage/root the udder for a time with their snouts. The sow either allows this or rolls onto her stomach.

In the wild

During the first two or three days of life, a wild boar sow stays continuously with her piglets in the nest. After this, the piglets remain in the nest while the sow forages in the vicinity. From day 6 the piglets accompany their mother, foraging for food. On day 7 she leaves the nest for good and rejoins the group around day 10.
Start to supplement the piglets' food from around day 7.

Signals of sufficient milk

Sow signal

The sow lies stretched out with a leg on a bar. This is a sign that she is feeling well and enjoying suckling. On the first day the piglets are still working out the suckling hierarchy.

Piglet signal

Photo: Varkens KI Noord-Brabant/Topics

Peacefully suckling, glistening piglets with plump backs. Black spots on the bridge of the nose are from the milk that splashes onto their noses when the milk lets down.

Signals of insufficient milk

Sow signals

A limp, poorly-filled udder.

The sow on the right is lying on her stomach, while the other sows are suckling. She has insufficient milk and is protecting her udder from her biting piglets.

Piglet signals

A lot of knee damage is a signal that the piglets are searching for scarce milk, that the floor is too rough, or both.

This udder has been damaged by agitated, rooting and biting piglets. The rear teats have come off worst. The piglets will work the udder for milk even while the sow is standing. They will respond fiercely, especially if there is a sudden drop in milk production.

The process

Benchmarks

Is this sow giving plenty of milk? How much milk did this sow give during farrowing? Besides wanting to know whether sow and piglets are eating and drinking properly at a specific time, you also need to be sure that these animals will continue to eat and drink properly.

'Properly' means not only that the animals remain healthy, but also that the piglets grow optimally and that the sow provides enough milk. To determine this, you can use benchmarks that provide information over a longer period, such as weekly feed intake, growth during the farrowing period and mortality rate.

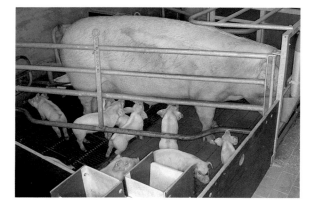

Measuring water

How do you know if a sow is drinking enough? A water meter provides certainty. The sow drinks at least 20 litres per day, depending on the ambient temperature. If the animal stands up easily and eats her feed, if her dung is not too hard, if the piglets get sufficient milk and if the drinker nipple provides sufficient water (≥ 2/l per minute) she is probably drinking enough.
Piglets suckling from a standing sow is a sign that the sow is giving little milk.

Weighing feed

The quantity of feed that a sow eats tells you her actual intake of energy and nutrients. After every feed, check whether the feeding system is actually delivering the set amount.

Weighing piglets

Production in the farrowing house is all about the growth of the piglets. Good growth tells you that piglets are drinking plenty of milk; poor growth indicates a disappointing milk intake.
The development of the piglets – gloss and musculature – gives an idea of their intake, but weighing them provides the most reliable information. The best measurement is the weight of a litter at weaning. Set goals on your farm which are both challenging and feasible.

Risk groups as a control

Checking risk groups is the best way to monitor feed intake and other factors. Because these groups require lots of attention, you can also use them to test your own management skills.

High-risk piglets: runts. Risks include high mortality and extra work. What is the percentage of light piglets? How light are they? How do these piglets perform in terms of mortality, growth, disease? Is there a standard procedure for dealing with runts? Should you give more attention to preventing runts? Piglets weighing less than 800 grams have little chance of survival.

High-risk sows: gilts. Risks include problems with farrowing, feed intake, savaging and milk production. How do the gilts and their piglets perform in terms of growth, mortality and disease? Does your gilt management require improvement?

High-risk sows: old animals. Risks include small litters and wide variation in birth weights. How many piglets in a litter, how much do they grow? Should you have replaced the sow earlier or can you be more flexible?

Know yourself

Working in the farrowing house means providing care to many sows and piglets. This requires precision and patience with every animal. Some people are naturally very meticulous and attentive and work carefully. Others are less so. They should be more deliberate in their actions. If you know yourself well, you can play up your strengths and make sure your weak points do not work to your disadvantage.

Mean and deviation

On average, these groups of piglets are the same weight. Conclusion: you need to know both the mean and the differences (deviation) before you can evaluate specific processes, such as growth in the farrowing house.

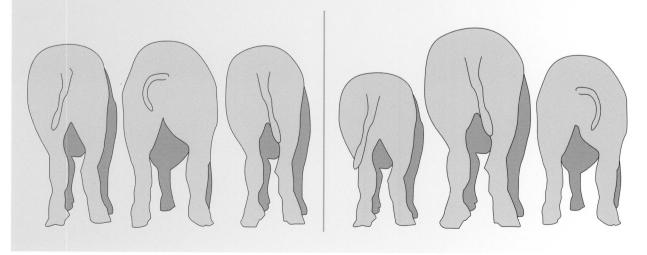

Light Feed Water Air
Peace Space
& quiet
Health

The right environment

Light

Pigs are diurnal animals. In the wild they live mainly in woods and rarely emerge into full sunlight.

Day length affects their reproductive rhythm and may also affect eating behaviour and milk production. Moreover, sufficient light is essential for working properly in the farrowing house. The stockman must be able to see everything clearly and must feel comfortable.

After the teat order has been determined the piglets will rarely fight any longer. To ensure efficient use of pen space, the various sections are filled with the most uniform possible groups of weaners and finishers. If groups of pigs must be mixed together, this should take place during the farrowing period, when piglets fight the least. But they do fight, so there are still adverse consequences for feed intake and infection risks.

Handling pigs in a calm and confident fashion ensures peace in the pens and peaceful animals. This results in very low stress and prevents many problems, which pays off in terms of better growth, fewer diseases and lower mortality.

In the wild

Wild boar produce litters of four to eight hairy piglets in March-April. A sow weighs 110-120 kg. Domestic pigs farrow year round, with litters ranging from 10 to 18 hairless piglets. Adult sows weigh 200-240 kg. After about four days, the piglets start exploring and begin to play. In the fourth week their playful behaviour reaches a peak.

40

Lying area with a comfortable microclimate

Piglets that are feeling cold lie curled up on their stomachs. They crawl close to heat sources such as other piglets or the sow's udder. If the ambient temperature is too low, a piglet feels cold. The right temperature depends on factors inherent to the piglet. First, its size. Larger piglets have a relatively smaller surface area so do not cool down as quickly. Second, the thickness of its back fat and, third, its feed intake (= fuel).

Moisture means danger. Wet areas quickly chill the piglet nest, and piglets with wet skin also cool down more quickly. Wet piglets need an ambient temperature 6°C higher.

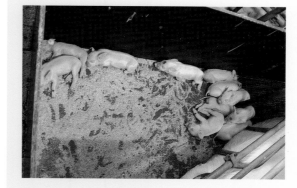

Too hot

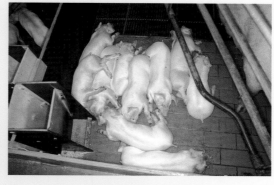

Just right

Too cold

The piglets are lying comfortably but the sow appears to be too warm. She is lying on her chest, mostly on the slats to minimise her contact with the warm floor. Sows use their breathing to cool themselves so need to take in fresh air through the nose.

A sick piglet needs a higher ambient temperature to feel comfortable. Make sure the piglet nest is warmer if the litter is sick. This will help the animals to recover. Also provide drinking water in dishes so they do not become dehydrated.

Disease-free, a good beginning

Nursery pigs undergo a large number of procedures and treatments. Some are necessary for their health, such as iron injections and disease treatments. Tail docking and teeth clipping also ensure the health of piglet and sow, although teeth clipping is usually unnecessary. And from the piglet's point of view, castration and ear tagging are nothing but stress. These procedures cause an immediate reduction in food intake. All treatments should affect the piglet as little as possible because this is the most vulnerable period of its life.

Pain means that piglets drink less, stand less and lie down more.

Diseases call for quick recognition and treatment. Further transmission must be prevented, so isolate sick animals, clean and disinfect materials and pens carefully and ask yourself the question: can I prevent this in future?

Organise routine treatments efficiently and conduct them carefully from beginning to end. The costs of an excellent tooth grinder and tail docker are minimal compared with the benefits of pleasant and efficient work. Evaluate the quality of your methods and tools regularly.

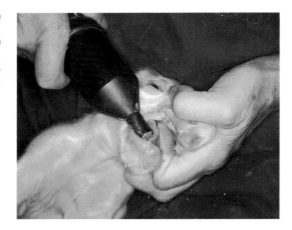

Look-think-act

What has gone wrong here? How do you intervene now and prevent this in future?

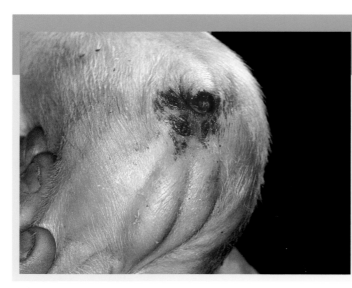

The wound is bleeding excessively and will remain open too long. Improve the tail docking procedure. This piglet has diarrhoea, which means it has lowered resistance. It is sick and cannot be operated on. Disinfect the wound and administer an antibiotic to support healing.

Signs of good procedures

Good wounds are dry, with little or no swelling and no redness. However, these tails have been docked too short. This causes an unnecessarily large wound which heals more slowly. It also leads to a greater risk of abscesses in the spinal cord.

Improvement necessary

Infections caused by procedures that have been carried out incorrectly are the tip of the iceberg. They are a sign that too many piglets are suffering unnecessarily.

This piglet's nose is swollen. A wound caused by incorrect tooth grinding has led to an inflammation of the upper jaw.

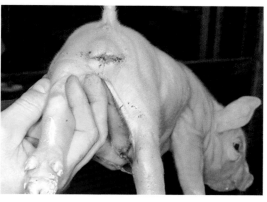

A swollen castration wound. The hind legs are also swollen.

Injuries

A strong piglet appears to recover without problems. But even this animal is losing resistance and growth, and becoming susceptible to other diseases.

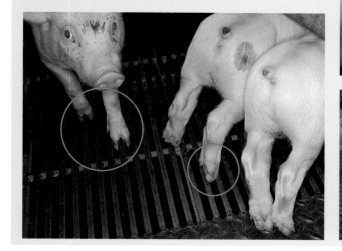

Piglets injure their hooves on rough floors, sharp slats and slats spaced too far apart. Agitation increases the number of wounds and their seriousness.

A weak piglet is struggling to overcome a wound infection. An abscess forms. This piglet should have been treated with antibiotics.

Preparation for weaning

Weaning is a risk moment, so requires good preparation.

During the fourth week, the protective effect of the colostrum begins to disappear. Increasingly, the piglet's own immune system has to take over. As a result the animal becomes especially susceptible to pathogens for several weeks. During weaning and for a few weeks afterwards, protect piglets from infections as far as possible.

The main sources of infection on a farm are sick pigs, older piglets and sows. In addition make sure that the piglets' resistance stays as high as possible. This means paying extra attention to feed and water intake, maximum rest and sufficient comfort. Provide clean, dry pens with an excellent climate and fresh, appetising feed that is offered in the same way as in the farrowing house.

Euthanasia (painless killing) is a useful intervention to ensure welfare. Failing piglets should be put out of their suffering in good time. If this abscess fails to heal after treatment, it may be best to euthanase the piglet as quickly as possible.

Picture puzzle
What do you see?

The lying piglets all have well-filled stomachs and intestines, round backs and glistening coats. The standing piglet has an empty belly and is seeking food.

For some reason this animal is not drinking enough milk. It may be sick or have an abnormality. Perhaps it cannot get to a good teat.

Culling of sows

At the end of the farrowing period, you must answer this question for each sow: will this animal be able to farrow and raise another litter of eleven to twelve piglets without problems?
A sow with problems should be culled in good time. Forty percent replacement generally means an ideally productive breeding herd.

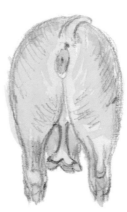

Consider the quality of the udder. Will the unsuckled teats still give milk during the next lactation? The udder suspension is much too weak.

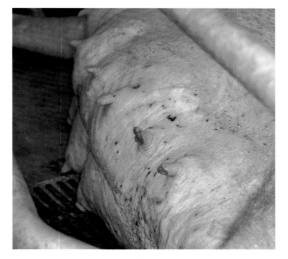

The piglets have damaged these teats beyond repair. Milk production was probably low. These are two reasons to cull the sow.

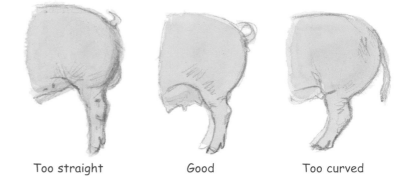

Too straight   Good   Too curved

When culling animals, also consider their leg quality; the sow should be able to stand properly (and so eat and drink easily).

Culling = prevention

The pressure sore on the shoulder signals that this sow has pain when she lies down. This is because she is very thin and no longer has any muscle or subcutaneous fat. Lameness, disease or other problems could be the cause. Give her something soft to lie on, such as a rubber mat.
Prevent other sows from having the same problems by paying attention to their back fat/general condition and mobility (culling). Determine the percentage of sows with skin injuries.

Diseases

The basic principle is the same for all diseases and disorders: the sooner you begin treatment, the smaller the damage. It makes sense to recognise diseases as early as possible and then treat them quickly and effectively.

The most common cause of a specific clinical picture and the best treatment can differ between farms. Invest in a good working relationship with a vet, so that he or she can advise you on a tailor-made treatment plan.

This udder is bulging out and the limits of the udder tissue are clearly visible. The teats feel hard. The piglets have not received much milk. The sow's body temperature is elevated (above 39.5°C).

This sow has a purulent discharge soon after farrowing, combined with swelling and an injury to the vulva. There appears to be an inflammation of the vagina and/or uterus. This is often caused by injury to the interior wall, probably from farrowing assistance but sometimes by the birth process itself. Treat the sow with antibiotics. If the sow has a fever and is eating less, supportive treatment is necessary.

Look-think-act
What do you see here?

There is vomit on the floor, consisting of curdled milk. There is also thick, yellow diarrhoea and one pig has diarrhoea around its anus. The three piglets in the foreground have empty bellies, probably due to vomiting and diarrhoea. The piglet with its belly on the rail has a full stomach. The piglets have therefore suckled. Possible causes include:

● rotavirus infection
● allergic reaction (after injections)
● other viral infections.

Additional tests, observing the disease progression and/or the reaction to treatment will help you track down the cause.

Piglets with diarrhoea

Dehydration is the greatest hazard with diarrhoea. Dishes of drinking water or an electrolyte solution reduce this risk. Refresh the electrolyte solution every two hours; bacteria can grow in it very quickly. Bacterial growth is slower in clean water

Thin, yellow diarrhoea in a two-week old piglet. The most probable cause is coccidiosis. Piglets become emaciated but rarely die.

Diarrhoea chart

The type of diarrhoea in piglets is often age-related. The chart shows types, causes, treatment and prevention. Care measures include piglet nests with optimal comfort, electrolyte solution and animal-oriented care. The basic principle is the same for all diseases: prevent the transmission of pathogens from sick animals.

Susceptible period	Description	Cause	Treatment	Prevention
From day 1	Neonatal scours	*E. coli*	Antibiotics and care	Vaccination of sow; colostrum intake; microclimate of farrowing pen; farm hygiene and farrowing pen hygiene.
From day 2-3	Bloody diarrhoea	*Clostridium perfringens*	Antibiotics and care	Clean and disinfect the farrowing pen; vaccinate sow.
From day 3	Yellow diarrhoea	Rotavirus	Fluid intake and care	Colostrum intake; clean and disinfect farrowing pen; prevent transmission from sick piglets.
Day 7-14	Coccidiosis	*Isospora suis*	Care	Preventive anti-coccidial agent; clean and disinfect farrowing pen thoroughly.

Greasy pig disease (exudative epidermitis) is caused by the Staphylococcus hyicus bacterium, which is carried by the sow. Piglets with low resistance develop this disease, as do piglets from gilts with few specific antibodies in their colostrum. It usually starts with skin injuries. Here, the damp spot on the nose is the starting point. Treat affected piglets with antibiotics. Disinfect wounds, especially fight wounds.

Ten points for inspection in sows in the farrowing pen

1 Alertness, posture, general impression, feed trough empty?

2 Availability of water (nipple provides 1.5 – 2 litres per minute).

3 Feed intake: quantity, feed not spoiled, does the sow stand up enough?

4 Dung: glistening, well-formed, soft.

5 Urine: colour and pus, flow.

6 Colour of skin, wounds.

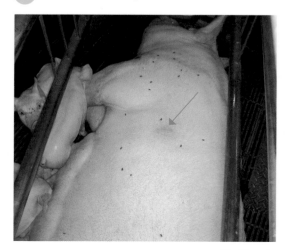

7 Udder condition: temperature, tenderness, hard/soft, lumps.

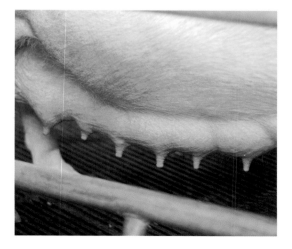

8 Body temperature: normal temperature is 38.5-39.0°C, higher in a warm environment. Above 39.5°C probably means a fever.

9 Respiration rate:12-30/min. Respiration increases due to problems with the airways and higher body temperature (fever, pen is too hot).

10 Noticeable abnormalities such as vomiting, shyness, excessive swelling of the belly, rash.

When making decisions, take the history of the sow (sow chart!) and hereditary factors (stress resistance) into account.

Ask your vet for a farm treatment plan.

Points for inspection in piglets

Inspect the litter (uniform?) for the following:

1 **Mean and deviation in terms of:**

- size
- colour, sheen and hair covering
- stomach fill, intestinal fill
- soundness and health of skin, hoofs, tails, possible injuries
- soiling

2 **Lying behaviour: warmth-seeking, cold-seeking**

3 **Behaviour: restful, playful, no aggression**

4 **Unclassified notable observations (UNOs)**

5 **Check every piglet for:**

- Alertness, general impression.
- Posture: does not act chilled, fearful, arched back (stomach ache?).
- Skin: glistening pink, no injuries.
- Any wounds heal quickly.
- Feed intake and water intake: well-filled belly, well-fleshed.
- Soiling: clean piglets.
- Joints: dry, not swollen, not painful.
- Notable observations.

Standard values for piglets

Heart rate	50 beats per minute
Respiration	30 breaths per minute
Temperature	38°C

Attention to the workplace

Quality of work and pleasure in your work are things that you can control. Make sure you have plenty of light, excellent materials and a good work area. Know what you are doing and why.

This is an example of a simple work area for castrating piglets. Everything is at the right working heigh. The knife is new and is placed in disinfectant; the cloth contains an alcohol-based disinfectant.

Picture puzzle
What do you notice about these piglets?

Piglet 1 has an empty belly. This piglet needs care because it is not eating and drinking enough. Why did this happen? Piglet 2 is paler than the others. This piglet needs attention because it may be falling sick. Piglets 3, 4 and 5 are glistening. They have plump backs and full bellies and are doing well.

Becoming pregnant

Photo: Marcel Bekken

The fact that pigs can produce piglets all year around makes them very suitable for animal husbandry. Piglet production is still an important determinant of the results of a pig farm. The foundation for the results is laid in the service pen and is closely related to the skill of the stockman.

Are you doing the right things, and are you doing the right things correctly?

Skill and reproduction go together. To determine the best insemination moment, you have to observe the sow carefully. The results of insemination depend in turn on the skill of the inseminator.

But the results of skill in the service pen are also affected by other factors, such as the quality of the farrowing period. Management decisions also play an important role: sow genetics, the use of a teaser boar, sow culling, boar genetics and semen storage and processing.

In the wild

In the wild, mating usually takes place in late autumn, so that the piglets are born at the end of the winter. A roaming boar mates with the sow and then leaves. Mating with multiple boars can lead to a litter of piglets with different sires. The wild boar's reproductive cycle is seasonal, but also depends on the supply of food. Autumn brings acorns, a rich and much-loved food source. In years of plenty, sows farrow twice.

Reproductive organs

Knowledge about the structure and function of the reproductive organs is essential for a good understanding of mating, ovulation and fertilisation.

The boar

The preputial sac of a boar contains a mixture of urine, sperm and dead skin cells. The scent of this material contributes to the sexual appeal of the boar. The spiralling out of the penis takes place through a combination of swelling and expansion of the S bend.

1. Prepuce, shaft
2. Preputial sac
3. Penis
4. S-bend
5. Accessory sexual glands
*   (seminal vesicles, prostate,*
*   bulbourethral or Cowper's glands)*
6. Testicle
7. Epididymis
8. Bladder
9. Kidney

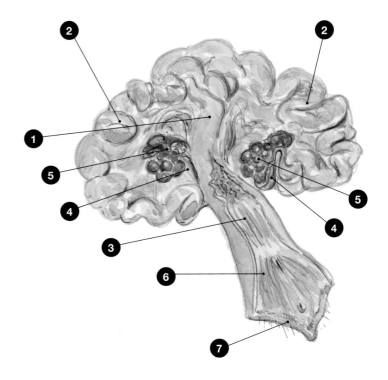

The sow

After service/insemination, the uterus contracts, pushing the sperm towards the oviduct, where fertilisation takes place. The large volume of semen makes this process possible. In non-pregnant sows, the distance from cervix to oviduct is 0.60 to 1 metre, in extreme cases up to 1.5 metres.
The embryos distribute themselves evenly around the uterus, sometimes moving from one horn of the uterus to the other.

1. Uterus
2. Horns of uterus
3. Cervix
4. Oviduct
5. Ovary
6. Vagina
7. Vulva

Lots of healthy piglets

The breeder's main aim is to produce the maximum number of healthy weaned piglets for the minimum effort and cost. From the pig's point of view, two keywords are important: lots and healthy. But having lots of piglets is not everything; they must also be vital. They must drink plenty of colostrum and get off to a strong start. After all, which is better: a litter of 12 strong piglets or a litter of 14 piglets with four weaklings? And what happens if there are more piglets than sow's teats?

The health and vitality of the piglets depends on various factors such as the pressure of infection on the farm and the genetics of the sow, boar and piglets. Management aspects also play a role, such as sow nutrition, insemination, housing and peace and quiet.

A healthy sow is a sow that is physically capable of producing 12 healthy piglets and feeding them properly until weaning. She has no infections or diseases that can prevent this and no wounds or disorders.

Lots!

Lots of eggs

The number of eggs released during ovulation increases until the fourth/fifth pregnancy. During the eighth pregnancy, the number of live-born piglets declines, while the number of still-borns increases. Emaciated sows produce fewer eggs; in practice, these are generally first-time farrowers.

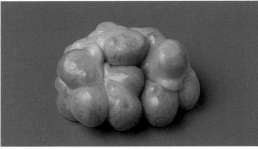

Photo: Janssen Animal Health

Lots of piglets

The estimated inheritance factor of litter size is 17%. This means that good genetics can achieve a lot. But it also means that management accounts for 83% of the variation in the number of piglets farrowed.

Inbreeding leads to smaller litters. Heterosis or 'hybrid vigour' (crossing non-related lines) increases litter size and the vitality of the piglets.

Lots of semen

The boar's penis ends in a corkscrew-like point. This is used to anchor the organ in the cervix so that the semen flows towards the uterus and does not return to the vagina. A single ejaculation produces 150 to 250 ml of semen. This is released in a sustained stream containing various fractions. The final fraction contains gelatinous 'plugs' which help to close off the cervix.

Determining condition

The condition of the sows at weaning is an excellent benchmark for nutrition and fertility. The right condition is a goal and a control point.
Physical condition predicts the ease with which a sow will raise her piglets in the farrowing house. Moreover, sows that have become too emaciated in the farrowing house do not come into oestrus properly and produce fewer live piglets.

To the eye

People with a practised eye can judge the condition of sows very accurately if they regularly 'calibrate' themselves by measuring the back fat. By placing your hand on the hip bone and spine, you can feel the thickness of the back fat.

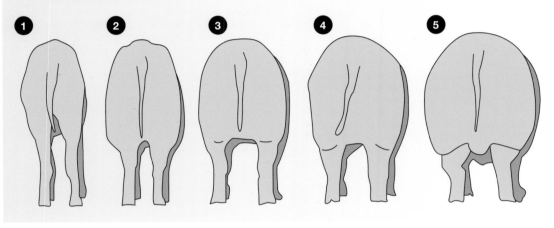

Measuring fat thickness

A fat thickness measurement provides the most reliable information about a sow's condition. Always measure at exactly the same location on the body and place the sensor at right angles to the animal with very little pressure on the skin. Standard values differ between breeding lines. The ideal is often around 18 mm of back fat when the sow enters the farrowing house. During the farrowing period, she should lose no more than 5 mm of back fat. For gilts at insemination, aim for 13 mm.

The measurement takes place over the last rib.

Determining the location with respect to the vertebrae. The dabs of scanning gel are placed 5.5 cm to the left and right of the spinal column.

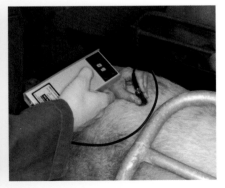

The sensor should be placed at right angles to the skin or it will give a false reading. The average of the two measurement points yields the back fat thickness of the sow. A measurement of 9 mm means the sow is too thin.

When to inseminate?

To determine the best time to inseminate, you must detect oestrus. The best time for insemination is up to 24 hours before ovulation. Ovulation takes place two-thirds of the way through oestrus, so you need to know the duration of oestrus in order to choose the right time for insemination. The duration of oestrus varies between farms and is between 30 and 60 hours. Within a farm the duration of oestrus remains reasonably constant, although shifts can take place during the year. Every farm can establish a standard insemination procedure by recording the duration of

oestrus and calculating the average. As part of this standard procedure, you can take account of the time between weaning and oestrus. Sows come into oestrus three to five days after weaning. Gilts have a shorter oestrus period than sows. The oestrus cycle of pigs lasts an average of 21 days, varying between 19 and 23 days. Sows which come into oestrus soon after weaning often have a longer oestrus period. Insemination after ovulation leads to fewer live-born piglets.

Oestrus signals

Pre-oestrus	Oestrus	Insemination	Over-insemination
Especially in gilts, the vulva is red and swollen. The vagina contains thick mucus.	Swelling of the vulva is reduced, the mucous membranes are pink. The vagina contains thin mucus.	After two-thirds of oestrus. This is often 24 hours after the sow's first standing reflex.	The sow still has a full standing reflex 16-18 hours after insemination.
The sow is agitated, cocks her ears and mounts other sows.	The sow typically makes a fairly soft, drawn-out, low-pitched grunt.		
The sow does not stand still if you press on her rump.	The sow stands and remains still for the boar. If you press on her rump, she stands completely still with an arched back.		

The standing reflex means that the sow stands rock-still with her ears cocked. She does this in response to pressure on her back and flank and stimulation from the boar (scent, sound, sight, contact).

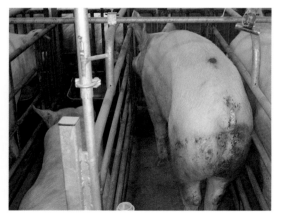

Oestrus begins when the sow displays the standing reflex for the stockman in the presence of a boar. This sow remains standing for the boar, without requiring further stimulation.

Stimulation by the boar

Before the boar mounts the sow, he nuzzles her flank and periodically lays his head on her rump. It is especially this foreplay, but also the mating by the boar, which improve the fertilisation results. Boar scent in spray cans, recorded boar sounds and stimulation by the stockman apparently cannot replace a real boar.

Boars take their time to mate, ranging from 5 to 15 minutes. An active boar spreads scent using glands on his fore feet and prepuce; he grinds his teeth, salivates and makes the typical boar sound. This staccato sound comprises a loud, hollow-sounding 'oh-oh-oh'. The more clearly a boar makes these signals, the more suitable he is as a teaser boar. Allowing a teaser to mate occasionally maintains his enthusiasm.

Sows and gilts become accustomed to the presence of a boar. So it is better not to have the boar around all the time, but allow intensive contact twice a day for 10 or 15 minutes.

The boar's extensive foreplay is a normal part of mating. It prepares the sow for mating/insemination.

Foto: Varkens-KI Noord-Brabant/Topigs

Direct contact with a teaser boar ensures that the sows indicate when they are in oestrus, produce better eggs and have stronger uterine contractions. This enables the sow to take up more semen and produce more vital piglets.

Fertilisation

The number of fertilised eggs per insemination is the result of the number of eggs released and their fertilisation rate.

The number of egg cells released during ovulation depends on the genetic characteristics of the sow and the management in the farrowing pen and service pen. Consider factors such as sow genetics and nutrition, feed intake, water intake and oestrus observation.

During a successful mating/insemination, 90% of the eggs are fertilised. To achieve this, both ovulation and fertilisation must proceed smoothly and effectively. If these processes do not proceed smoothly, this means that oestrus is not proceeding properly and results in a poor correlation between ovulation, fertilisation and the implantation of the embryos in the uterus.

Insemination

Work calmly and hygienically. Take the time to stimulate the sow by pressing on her rump and flank. Use disposable pipettes.

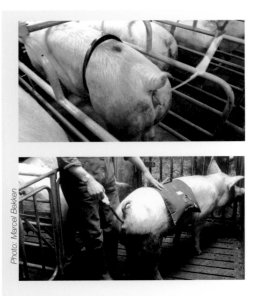

Photo: Marcel Bekken

Imitating the boar

During artificial insemination you should imitate the boar as closely as possible. A mating frame applies pressure to the sow's flanks and a sandbag pushes down on her loins. Continue to stimulate for 15 minutes after insemination, with the pipette in the vagina and the boar in front of the sow.

Instructions for insemination with a foam pipette

Step 1.

Clean the vulva, for example with a disposable towelette. Take a clean pipette and apply a suitable lubricant.

Step 2.

Slide the pipette slowly into the sow's vagina. Turn a *spiral-shaped* pipette counter clockwise until you feel firm resistance. The point is now in the cervix. Pull the pipette back slightly so that it can empty properly. You should push a *button-shaped* pipette into the proper location in the cervix.

Step 3.

Connect the sperm container to the pipette and hold it upside down so that it can empty. Give the sow plenty of time to take up the semen. This can easily take 10 minutes.

If the insemination takes place correctly with a standard dose of semen (two to three billion sperm cells), the flow-back of semen during and after insemination has little effect on the fertilisation results.

Cervix

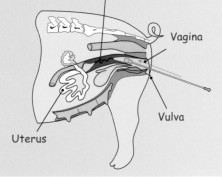

Vagina

Vulva

Uterus

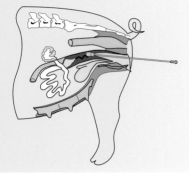

Pregnant or not?

After insemination, you need to determine which sows are not pregnant as quickly as possible be-cause 'empty' sows require extra attention, first of all to get them into oestrus again. But there may also be something wrong with their uterus or ovaries, and you must ascertain this as early as possible.

Various methods have been used in the past to detect sow pregnancy. Today, this is usually done with an ultrasound examination. Beginning 19 days after insemination or mating, ultrasound gives a reliable indication of pregnancy. A second test after 14 days will indicate any early aborters.

For pregnancy checks, an ultrasound examination can be made from day 19.

From six weeks, the belly of a pregnant sow begins to bulge obviously. If in doubt, do an ultrasound.

Pig signals should answer the following questions

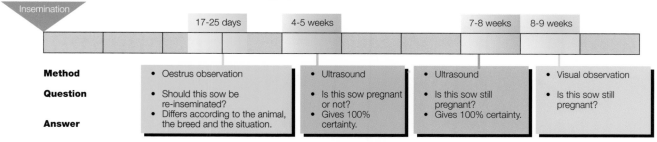

	17-25 days	4-5 weeks	7-8 weeks	8-9 weeks
Method	• Oestrus observation	• Ultrasound	• Ultrasound	• Visual observation
Question	• Should this sow be re-inseminated?	• Is this sow pregnant or not?	• Is this sow still pregnant?	• Is this sow still pregnant?
Answer	• Differs according to the animal, the breed and the situation.	• Gives 100% certainty.	• Gives 100% certainty.	

A good oestrus check three weeks after insemination will always be essential.

What do you see on an ultrasound?

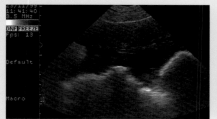

The uterus of a pregnant sow, 21 days after insemination. The uterus lies like a long snake in the belly containing the amniotic sacks (elongated sacks of amniotic fluid with an embryo). Depending on how the ultrasound images the sacks, they can appear circular, oval or randomly curled.

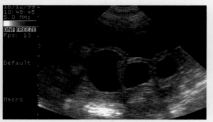

The same pregnancy at day 23. The amniotic sacks have already grown a great deal and become longer. Because the uterus is coiled, you sometimes see multiple circles next to each other which are different cross-sections of the same sack.

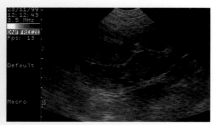

An image from day 35. The wall of the uterus and the placenta have thickened and have grown tightly together. The embryo is in the middle.

Images: Esaote-Pie Medical

Light Feed Water Air
Peace
& quie   Space

Health

Other conditions

In the service pen, the basic needs must also be satisfied: feed-water-light-air-peace & quiet-space and health. The working conditions should also be optimal so that everyone can work well and enjoy their work.

Water must be plentifully available and the sows must have enough to eat. Excellent feed provision before and during oestrus promotes strong ovulation. This is due to the hormone insulin, which is released when the blood sugar level is elevated. This effect is clearest in gilts and first-time farrowers. The temperature in the service pen should not be too high or too low. Around 18°C is good, with few fluctuations and measured with a reliable thermometer or sensor near the sows. The air in the pen must be fresh and clean, free of manure fumes.

Peace & quiet

Avoid stress between the third day and the fourth week after insemination. Do not move sows during this period. The level of stress depends on the handling of the sows and their familiarity with the conditions. Immediately after servicing, increase the feed to improve the condition of thinner sows.

Light

Enough light near the heads of sows and gilts stimulates oestrus. A standard level is 100 lux. People also need more light to do their work pleasantly and well. Maintain a regular day-night rhythm of 14 to 18 hours of light by using a timer. Clean the lamps every four weeks because a pig barn is dusty and flies quickly soil the lamps. And keep the windows clean.

Risk group: gilts

Gilts form a separate group in the service pen. Gilts require special attention; for a gilt, almost everything is new. She has never come into oestrus before, is unfamiliar with the service pen and doesn't know the sows. Moreover, gilts do not always come into oestrus easily.

Insemination moment

Gilts reach puberty at about 25 weeks. The exact time depends on their growth, the season, the breed and their health.

The weight of the gilt is the best calibration point for insemination. A suitable time for insemination is when the gilt weighs 140 kg during her third oestrus. Stress causes gilts to come into oestrus. Stimulate this process by providing intensive contact with the boar twice a day for 15 minutes, but no longer; this is counter-productive. Record the oestrus. Give the gilt two weeks of rest, then stimulate her to come into oestrus again.

This gilt is attempting to turn around in her box. The animal is not familiar with this environment and may be unfamiliar with the sow next to her. Because she is relatively small, she has enough space to make the attempt. She hooks her head behind the vertical rail, which gives her enough grip to exert force. There is a risk she will become trapped, strangle herself or lose piglets.

Picture puzzle
What do you notice about this gilt?

This gilt is lame. She stands and walks with an arched back and favours her left fore leg. And she stands with her back legs tucked under her body. Trauma is the probable cause, due to an abrupt movement. There is a good probability that this happened when she mounted, or was mounted by, a gilt in oestrus.

Weaned piglets

A weaned piglet or weaner has a tremendous capacity for growth, but is also very vulnerable. If the animal receives excellent housing and care, this is rewarded with healthy growth. On the other hand, shortcomings quickly result in problems. Are you doing the right things, and are you doing the right things correctly?

With their incredible capacity for growth, healthy piglets are a pleasant surprise every day.

Many things that apply to weaners also apply to finishers, so make sure you read Chapter 6 as well.

In the wild

During the second week of life, the sow and piglets leave their nest. Piglets begin to eat different food and become acquainted with other piglets.
The animals get to know each other mostly during the third and fourth weeks, especially from nose-to-nose contact. They fight very little and biting and rooting under the belly are almost unknown. When the piglets are four weeks old, they are already eating substantial quantities of roughage such as grass. The time when they are completely weaned differs greatly between piglets in a litter, ranging from 9 to 17 weeks. Piglets who suckled during the first days on productive teats are weaned later than piglets who received less milk initially.

Drastic changes

From one moment to the next, a weaner experiences a big transition. Not only does his feed change, but the way in which his food is provided is also completely different. Equally unexpected, the animal finds itself in new surroundings with new herd mates.

Do not wean too early. If this is necessary due to the lack of active nipples on the sow, the artificial sow is an alternative. This enables piglets to drink milk replacer so that weaning can be postponed for a time.

Lowered immunity

The protection from colostrum, maternal immunity, begins to decline rapidly from the fourth week. The piglet must now protect itself against the bacteria, viruses and mycoplasmas he continuously encounters. Many pathogens (PRRS, circo) are present in large numbers on a farm because they repeatedly infect weaned piglets. They jump from one vulnerable group to the next. To keep pigs healthy on a farm, it is essential to break this cycle of transmission. By strictly separating batches of pigs using an all-in/all-out system, organising walking routes from young pigs to older pigs and maintaining strict hygiene, you can achieve this aim. In addition, you must always keep their immunity as high as possible. This means optimal feeding, water intake, ideal ambient temperatures and maximum peace and quiet. And vaccinate if necessary. The lesser a pig gets ill, the fewer pathogens it will spread.

When two groups mix, the dominant pigs are the first ones to fight for position. Then the 'number two' pigs fight and so forth. When mixing multiple groups, this becomes more difficult. Pigs that are equally matched have to fight a long time before a winner emerges. Low-ranking pigs tend to give in quickly.

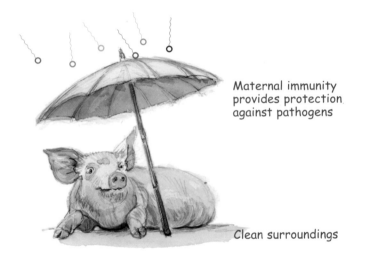

Maternal immunity provides protection against pathogens

Clean surroundings

In segregated early weaning, the piglets are weaned early (21 days) and moved immediately to a clean, new pen. At that time they are still protected by an umbrella of immunity from the colostrum, and few pathogens are lurking in the new pen.

Large groups of animals have more disease problems because there is more transmission of pathogens. This is due to the larger number of meetings between a larger number of pigs. This can be calculated using the transmission factor: $(N^2) - N$, where N is the number of pigs. With five pigs the transmission factor is $(5^2) - 5 = 20$, with twenty pigs it is 380, and with forty pigs it is 1,560. The transmission factor therefore increases exponentially with the number of pigs.

The first day

Weaning is a clear example of a risk moment. The saying 'preparation wins the war' is never more true than it is here. Successful weaning begins with a top-notch pen that is ready to receive the piglets with full hospitality, and with piglets that are ready to be weaned. By changing as few things as possible during weaning, you reduce stress. For example, do not move the piglets.

Success factors in weaning

Success factors are things you have to do to achieve good results, but you can call them anything you like.

The following success factors apply to weaning:
- Begin with healthy, disease-free piglets.
- Every piglet has a generous feed and water intake.
- No piglet is too cold or too hot.
- Every piglet has a quiet place to rest.
- The pen is clean, completely dry, comfortable and free of risk.
- No diseases are brought in to the pen.

Check every piglet carefully at least twice daily for feed intake and health. Make sure you can intervene easily if required. In fact, this is also a success factor: early and effective intervention if something goes wrong.

During the first three days, keep the light on round the clock. This will encourage the piglets to begin eating sooner and eat and drink more. Start the animals off at 26-28°C and reduce this to 25°C in the second week. Check the floor temperature, the temperature near the piglets and the airflow.

The piglets must be able to find food and water very easily. Are they familiar with the feed trough and the nipple drinker? Providing water in open dishes stimulates intake and piglet health. Feed troughs of liquid feed also promote a good start.

Virtually all farm-linked diseases are transmitted by older pigs to younger ones, so the compartment must be completely empty and clean when the new piglets arrive. But they can also acquire pathogens along the way, so keep a critical eye on your working methods.

Feed intake

It is crucial for the health of the piglet that it should continue to eat. If it stops eating, it runs a greater risk of hypothermia, bowel oedema (E. coli) and streptococcal meningitis.

The risk group comprises piglets that drank a lot of milk before weaning. In the farrowing house, these animals ate little solid food and are therefore faced with the biggest transition. They are also the biggest, most dominant piglets so have to fight a great deal. This is why it is often the best-looking piglets that develop bowel oedema.

Changes in eating

Eating from the sow:	Eating after weaning:
24-times per day	if the piglet wants to/can/dares
the sow is in control	the piglet has to act of its own accord
all at the same time	depends on the eating space
warm	ambient temperature
liquid: sucking	solid (pellet or liquid feed): eating

Eating

Piglets like to eat at the same time. Seeing other piglets eat makes them want to eat. Feeding systems where all piglets can eat simultaneously help them get off to a good start. Do not place feed and water in dark corners, put them in the light.

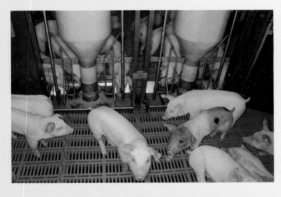

Although most weaned piglets will start eating within a few hours, it can be more than two days before all piglets have started eating. Make sure all piglets can get to the feed easily, because it is the poor eaters who will have problems.

Isolation pens allow weak piglets to have extra appetising food and warmer surroundings. The quiet, safe surroundings also contribute to feed intake and general recovery.

Feed and water
Composition of the feed

Both the feed and the water given to the pigs must have the right composition. This is a lot of work. First of all, the levels of nutrients must be correct, as well as the digestibility, for every feeding, for every pig. Does the last piglet get the same feed as the big piglet who gets there first? Actually, the small piglets need something extra.

Water!

Feed and water must not contain any contaminants and must not be spoiled. Weaners eat and drink relatively little in the first few weeks, so pipelines flow slowly and spoilage can occur. Water from a private supply must be tested at least once a year. But all kinds of spoilage can take place in water lines in pens. Algae thrive above 20°C. Fungi flourish in medicated lines. Storage vats easily become contaminated.

This trough contains wet feed. It will spoil quickly, especially in the warm weaning compartments. Take a handful of feed from the storage bin and a handful from the feed trough and compare the moisture content.

Here the nipple drinker is located in a liquid feed trough, posing a risk that dominant pigs who want to drink will prevent other pigs from eating. The pig that is waiting has a poorly filled belly.

A separate drinking location and a correctly opened feed trough. Make sure the piglets clean up the trough but still get enough to eat.

Weaned piglets must always have access to feed or they must all be able to eat a full meal simultaneously. The latter is very difficult to organise. Giving liquid feed to weaned piglets requires a great deal of skill; dry feed is much easier.

Peace & quiet
The number of pigs in a pen
The housing costs of large groups are lower but their feed conversion is usually higher. This may have to do with their higher activity.

Large groups are difficult to inspect properly. Because there are so many pigs walking around, it is difficult to get a proper overview. And if you notice one pig, it is more difficult to mark the animal or treat it. Twelve piglets in a group would appear to be the maximum.

Space
Growing fast
Weaners grow from almost 10 kg to 25 kg. In the beginning the pen is very roomy, but at the end it may be tight for space. As it becomes more crowded the feed may become less accessible, leading to declining growth. In a very crowded pen, the pigs have more difficulty getting to the feed and water. *Whittemore (1998) calculated the minimum floor area as follows: 0.050 x body weight0.65. At 25 kg, this is 0.40 m².*

Pen climate
Sufficient feed intake is required for piglets to keep their body temperature at the correct level. In the first few days after weaning, they eat little and the pen temperature must be higher. But later on, piglets that eat poorly get cold more quickly than those that eat well.

Bear in mind that wet floors and draughts increase the chill factor. Adjust the pen temperature so the smallest piglet is comfortable.

In large groups, there are more leg problems and it is more important to intervene early. The danger that lame pigs will eat too little is greater than in smaller groups

Small piglets lose more heat than larger ones. Fat insulates and eating more ensures more heat production.

Look-think-act
What do these pigs tell you?

These pigs have empty bellies, narrow backs and are getting long hair. The animals are eating little, not growing well and are cold. There could be many causes. Disease, inadequate feed, incorrect feed, contaminated drinking water. Remove the suspected cause and check the condition of the animals.

Inspecting piglets

Some people are naturally tuned in to pig signals, others less so. But everyone can learn to inspect pigs properly and can become better and better at doing so.

Inspect piglets from the large ones to the small ones. Start with the group, then the individual. And then go back to the group, comparing one pig with the other animals. Look to see if other pigs are giving out similar signals or signals that help you to form a complete picture.

View the pigs regularly from a different perspective. You get the best impression of the animals in the pen when you are in the pen yourself, at the same level as the pigs.

Large groups have more disease problems because there is more transmission of pathogens due to the larger number of meetings between larger numbers of pigs.

Better and better inspections

Train yourself to inspect more and more aspects. Is the skin blemish-free? Do I see traces of a healing skin infection or of skin irritation? How old is this piglet?

Has it been difficult or easy to achieve a uniform herd? Are there differences in uniformity? What kind of differences are there? Hair? Colour? Age? Ear damage? Type? Belly fullness?

Also pay attention to management signals. Are all the tails equally long? Are all the ear tags in the ears? Is there soiling? Dry joints? Hoof injuries?

Materials and organisation

Information is worthless if you don't use it. Make sure everything you see leads to a conclusion and follow-up action. 'This is good/not good and we are now going to do the following.'

Make time and provide facilities for proper inspection. And set money aside for supplementary tests, for example, on pigs that have died suddenly. What do these animals tell you?

An infrared thermometer measures the temperature at the place where the red light falls. This enables you to determine quickly, during an inspection, that the temperature of the floor is correct. This is an inexpensive and useful tool.

Animal inspection

During an animal inspection examine every pig from back to front, and from large to small. Concentrate on signs of health and recognise early signals of problems.

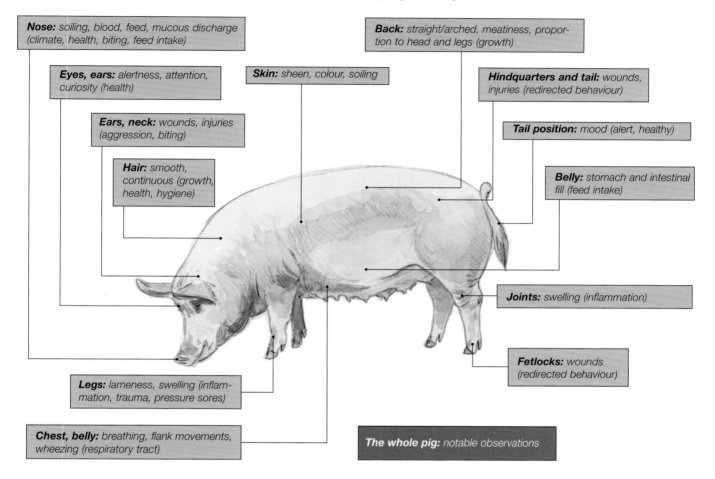

Nose: soiling, blood, feed, mucous discharge (climate, health, biting, feed intake)

Eyes, ears: alertness, attention, curiosity (health)

Ears, neck: wounds, injuries (aggression, biting)

Hair: smooth, continuous (growth, health, hygiene)

Skin: sheen, colour, soiling

Back: straight/arched, meatiness, proportion to head and legs (growth)

Hindquarters and tail: wounds, injuries (redirected behaviour)

Tail position: mood (alert, healthy)

Belly: stomach and intestinal fill (feed intake)

Joints: swelling (inflammation)

Fetlocks: wounds (redirected behaviour)

Legs: lameness, swelling (inflammation, trauma, pressure sores)

Chest, belly: breathing, flank movements, wheezing (respiratory tract)

The whole pig: notable observations

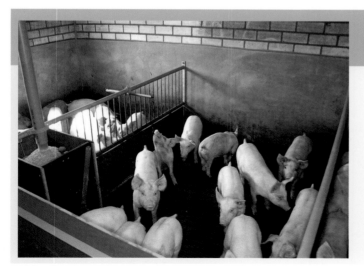

Picture puzzle
Which pig stands out?

If you look long enough, you notice something about several of the pigs. The one that stands out most is in the middle of the photograph with its hindquarters in the corner. The animal is standing with an arched back and is not responding to its surroundings. It may be defecating, but it could also have a problem.

Feed Water

Light   Air

Peace   Space
& quiet

Health

Diseases

There are many diseases that threaten weaners and finishers. To treat them effectively and to introduce effective prevention, the cause must be clear. Important diseases are diarrhoea and respiratory disorders. They can have various causes. An expert consultant is very important in the battle against disease. He or she can prevent 'farm blindness' and point out signals and solutions. Too often, a name is assigned to a clinical picture or a standard treatment is begun too quickly, with the risk of incorrect treatment and spreading disease. A good vet or consultant queries his own conclusions and approach on a regular basis. He checks his actions by conducting lab tests and by continuing his education.

Diarrhoea

The cause of diarrhoea is difficult to determine based on disease symptoms. A vet incorporates much more information into an examination and bases his decision partly on his knowledge of the farm and his experience.

Diarrhoea signals and diagnoses

Appearance of faeces	Pig symptoms	Time of occurrence	First impression	Final diagnosis
Thin faeces	Sluggish, eating less, no fever.	At any time	Feed-related diarrhoea	
Watery	No fever. Not eating, crawling together. Sometimes bluish ears, nose, belly. Pig sometimes dies.	Several days to two weeks after weaning (or other feed changes)	Post-weaning diarrhoea (*E. coli*)	Post-mortem examination of untreated pig.
Thin, like hot chocolate	Fever (39.5 -40.5°C). Acute mortality.	At any time	Vibrio (*Brachyspira hyodysenteriae*)	Post-mortem examination of pig with typical clinical picture.
Thin, dark grey to blackish. Sometimes bloody	Fever (39.5 -40.5°C), pale. Sunken belly, especially in loin area.	Especially during the second half after the growing period.	PIA or PHE (*Lawsonia intercellularis*)	Post-mortem or post-slaughter examination of intestines.
Very watery, yellow	Sluggish, not eating, lying on each other. Fever (40.5 -41°C), sudden death.	At any time	Salmonella	Dung testing, post-mortem examination.

In pens with a full slatted floor, it is often difficult to detect diarrhoea early because the dung goes straight into the pit. If you see diarrhoea against the walls or on the pigs themselves, then you know for sure. Sick pigs will be paler and more sluggish, with sunken bellies.

Test your knowledge of diseases. What do you see? How did this happen? What can you do?

Clinical picture 1

This piglet is tilting its head upwards and rigidly cocking its ears. The cause is meningitis. The resulting fluid build-up exerts pressure on the brain and causes muscular reactions such as pedalling. This head position maximises the volume of the skull and minimises the pressure. Streptococci (S. suis) probably caused the infection. These bacteria enter the bloodstream through wounds and can then cause meningitis and joint inflammation. If pigs are eating poorly, streptococci can enter the bloodstream from the intestines, for example after weaning.

Clinical picture 2

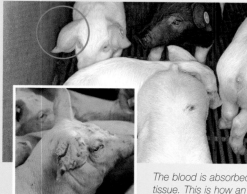

An aural haematoma is caused by a blood vessel rupturing in the ear. This can occur when a piglet flaps its ears due to fighting, if you lift the animals by their ears, or if an ear tag is not inserted properly. Piglets flap their ears when their ears itch inside, due to mange for example. In the beginning, haematoma of the ear is painful. The piglet tilts its head and remains at the side of the pen. Treatment is not necessary, but prevention is. Pain results in the piglet eating less. Itching causes agitation and uses energy.

The blood is absorbed by the body and is replaced, more or less, by connective tissue. This is how an aural haematoma turns into cauliflower ear. Remove ear tags because these may cause infection.

Clinical picture 3

Skin haemorrhages occur primarily on hindquarters, sometimes on the belly or in the axilla (armpit) or groin. This picture is compatible with PDNS or Porcine Dermatitis and Nephritis Syndrome, a disorder linked to the circo virus. The clinical picture is similar to swine fever.

Clinical picture 4

Photo: Mark Roozen

E. coli sepsis results in sunken eyes and a purple tinge to the point of the nose, tips of the ears and belly. Piglets with meningitis lift their heads up and pedal. But it could be caused by other problems such as Glässer's disease.

Respiratory disorders

The lungs and respiratory tracts of pigs are very vulnerable, partly because the lungs are small in proportion to the body, and also due to the continuous inhalation of dust and manure fumes and the widespread presence of certain respiratory pathogens. In terms of pig signals, once again there are many things you do not want to see: coughing, soiled eyes, runny noses, etc. If the pigs appear to have problems, you need to know the exact cause quickly. Only then can you determine the best treatment and the best prevention. But it is difficult, if not impossible, to make a diagnosis directly from the signals.

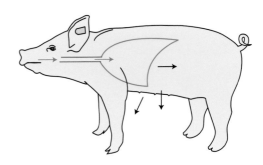

Inhalation takes place by lifting up the ribs and pushing down the diaphragm. The chest volume increases and the lungs fill with air.

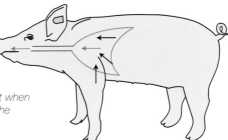

Exhalation takes place as the elastic lungs contract when the diaphragm and chest muscles relax. Tightening the abdominal and rib muscles amplifies the exhalation.

The origins of respiratory disorders

Signaal	Cause
Eyes	
Redness	Usually caused by irritating fumes and dust.
Swollen mucous membranes	Specific pathogens (including PRRS).
Tear staining	Blocked tear duct (atrophic rhinitis, swollen mucous membranes).
Nose	
Sneezing	Irritation of nasal cavity and throat. Usually caused by irritating dust or fumes.
Nasal discharge	Infection and/or irritation of nasal membranes.
Coughing	
Dry cough	Irritation by dust, irritating fumes. Infection of deep respiratory tract with little mucus or thick mucus.
'Wet' or productive cough	Infection of respiratory tract with copious mucus.
Repressed cough	Infection of respiratory tract with severe pain.
Deep cough	Roundworm infection.
Breathing	
Rapid breathing	Body temperature too high. Insufficient uptake of oxygen or exhalation of CO_2.
Flank movements	Inhalation obstructed by restricted airways or mucus.
Wheezing	Contraction of abdominal muscles on exhalation due to loss of lung elasticity (scar tissue).
General	
Wide-legged stance, head held down when coughing	Slackened abdomen due to pain from pleurisy.
Pale, poor appetite, sluggish	General disease (not necessarily related to respiratory disease).

Transmission of diseases

Besides the symptoms, the vet needs to know how many pigs are sick and how the disease has spread in the pens and sections. This makes it possible to identify possible types of pathogen.

- The disease spreads gradually through a pen and through the compartment. Every day, there are a few more sick pigs. This may be a bacterial infection.
- The disease spreads through the majority of the pigs in a pen over several days and then is transmitted almost as quickly through the section. This may be a viral disease, such as influenza. Viruses are spread quickly by moisture droplets in exhaled air, mucus, nasal discharge and coughing.

- Virtually all the pigs become sick very quickly. The cause may not be infectious, but a broken fan, for example. In that case, 'normal' respiratory bacteria cause the disease symptoms.

Viral infections usually cause acute, high fever (≥41°C). Bacterial diseases often proceed more slowly with a slightly lower fever.
With the exception of atrophic rhinitis, a definitive diagnosis cannot be made on the basis of symptoms alone. The farm vet can make the best evaluation and requires laboratory tests and post mortems for this purpose.

Signals of respiratory disorders

A runny nose. Pus is caused by inflammation, mucus by an irritation of the mucous membrane. The pig appears to be still active and is eating well. It is alert, has a full belly and glossy skin and its hair is smooth and continuous.

Head held low, belly slack and legs wide apart: all to prevent stress on the belly. This piglet probably has a great deal of pain when coughing due to pleurisy. It may produce mucus or pus when it coughs (productive cough).

This piglet appears to have a slight cough, probably a dry cough. The dirty eyes are caused by irritation of the mucous membrane and collected dust. The animal is pale and has a distended belly. The problem has existed for some time.

Finishing pigs

Finishing pigs or finishers are entering a new phase of life. The animals are transported to a new location and are often placed in new groups. This leads to agitation. New surroundings also mean new health hazards. By properly understanding behaviour, you can avoid problems.

Healthy pigs have pink, glistening skin, clean and alert eyes and relaxed behaviour and posture.

Many things that apply to finishers also apply to weaners, so make sure you read Chapter 5 as well.

In the wild

A young wild boar, a weaner, spends his days foraging, playing, resting and – occasionally – wallowing (taking a mud bath). Foraging largely determines the structure of the day.
Pigs are diurnal animals and begin the day with eating and exploration. However, they switch easily to a night rhythm. The most important reason for this is bad weather: pigs hate rain. A second reason is that they are hunted during the day.

Process management

Rearing finishers is both a project and a process. Projects have a beginning, an end and well-defined phases: setting in – starting – finishing – delivering. Processes are continuous activities: eating – drinking – resting – growing. At the end of the finishing period, it becomes clear how successful these processes have been. Feed conversion, growth per day and health can be expressed in numbers. In one sense this information comes too late, because you can't do anything to change what has already happened. On the other hand, you can learn a great deal from this information if you take the time and effort to analyse and compare the results and the process. Ultimately you want to be able to look ahead. "When I do this, than that will be the effect". This type of weaner pigs need this type of reception, this type of nutrition, and this type of care. You begin to understand the consequences of your actions. For example, you understand that weaner pigs require the processes of reception, nutrition and care. You recognise the signals when things are going well. And you see the signals that tell you to intervene.

Look forward with process evaluation

Starting material	Process	Resultaten
Quality of piglets	• Feed intake • Water intake • Health • Rest	• Slaughter weight • Meat percentage, back fat thickness, muscle thickness • Health of intestines, lungs, liver

Use the results of previous batches to improve the process of subsequent batches.

Chain of cause and effect

a farrowing sow eats poorly
↓
the piglets do not drink enough colostrum
↓
more disease problems occur in the farrowing house
↓
more disease in weaned piglets
↓
more problems after setting in finishing pigs

The basis for the health of finishing pigs begins with the pre-parturient sow in the farrowing house.

Management time

Take the time to write down and evaluate all the data from a batch of finishing pigs and to make plans for improvement.

Picture puzzle
What do you think?

Several pigs are drinking the urine of this urinating gilt. They may be thirsty. Check the water flow from the nipple drinkers/watering troughs. Liquid feed sometimes contains a lot of salt, causing pigs to drink a great deal of water. If they become seriously dehydrated, the pigs will stagger around as if drunk.

Everything in its place

The first day after setting in, the pigs have to get several matters in order. Besides feed and water intake, these include dominance hierarchy and layout of the pen and usage areas.

Feed intake is the same as in the case of weaners. Animals must be able to find the feed, they must have easy access to the feed and it should not be too different from the feed they are accustomed to.

Dominance hierarchy

When mixing pigs during setting in, you should always:

- Adapt feed and feed dosage to weight;
- Feed gilts and castrated males/boars separately;
- Aim to deliver pigs that are as uniform as possible;
- Get the maximum use from the pen area;
- Make inspections as easy as possible;
- Make group transport of piglets as easy as possible.

The disadvantages of mixing include the agitation that this causes and the injuries that occur. After mixing, pigs have a sustained higher body temperature, which indicates stress.

Providing sufficient space and escape possibilities ensures that fights for dominance result in a minimum of problems. After one day, the dominance ranking is established. Piglets from large groups (≥14) have fewer problems with mixing.

Determining pen layout/usage areas

After they enter a pen, the pigs choose a resting area, an eating area and then a defecating area. The eating area is determined by the position of the feed station, but the resting area is not. This area must provide peace and quiet, a comfortable climate and protection. Temperature and comfort therefore determine the choice of the resting area. Consequently, when the pigs enter the pen, the ventilation must be functioning properly, the pen temperature must be correct (24°C) and the floor must be dry. Fights caused by mixing can affect the decision-making process.

These finishers are easily viewed at rest through a window. The open partition next to the slats makes this corner unsuitable as a rest area because pigs from the other pen disturb their rest. In the middle section, they can lie undisturbed provided the climate is good. Although they prefer to defecate in a more protected area, the pigs will make the slatted floor their defecation area.

Slatted floor: cool/cold
Open sides: disturbance by other pigs from neighbouring pens.

Convex floor: warm
Solid, closed sides: protection, no disturbance by pigs from other pens.

Feed

Water

Slatted floor: cool/cold

A sketch of the pen in the photograph, seen from the pig's point of view. The path from the eating area to the defecating area is not shown. During setting in there will be enough space, but what will happen when the pigs weigh 80 kg or more? (See page 67, area calculation).

Pen soiling

Why does one batch of pigs defecate in the right place but not the other one? Pigs have two reasons for defecating in an undesired location. First of all, because they decide that a specific place is still the best. And secondly because they think the pen is too warm, so they create a 'mud bath'.

Defecation and urination

Pigs defecate facing the other pigs with their hindquarters safely protected, so they prefera corner with two solid walls. And a solid floor as well, because this causes fewer hoof injuries (pain).

Pigs experience urination differently than defecation. The animal leaves the resting area but won't always go all the way to the defecation area. It seeks less protection. Boars urinate almost everywhere.

Gilts have a stronger urge to keep their pen clean than boars and castrated males, possibly because boars tend to have more of a roaming nature.
At liquid feed troughs the floor becomes damp quickly, which invites the pigs to make it into a defecation area.
A step under the trough prevents the animals from defecating with their hindquarters against the trough and therefore in the trough

Wallowing (mud baths)

If pigs start to lie in their own manure, something is going wrong. Either they are too warm or they have too little space. For that matter, some pigs begin to wallow sooner than others.

Rest, redirected behaviour and aggression

Finishing pigs spend at least 80% of the day resting. This means that the individual animal and the group feel comfortable. This comfort comprises multiple aspects, such as a satiated feeling, a pleasant climate and lack of disturbance.

Agitation

Many things can disturb the peace and quiet. As long as the pig can return to a comfort situation, this is not serious. A brief period of agitation is then followed by peace and quiet. Stress occurs when the pig cannot control the conditions. The animal remains agitated and starts displaying redirected behaviour. Certain stress factors also cause aggression. For example, a pig hears that feeding is taking place and wants to eat. If it can eat enough, it will lie down peacefully again. But if it cannot eat, it will begin displaying redirected behaviour and become aggressive. Another example: there is a draught in the resting area. If the pigs can find a resting area without a draught, this is not serious. But if they can't, they will become aggressive and display redirected behaviour.

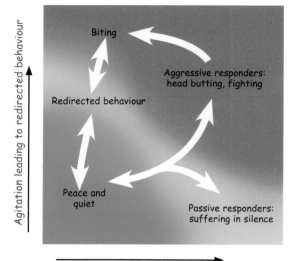

Pigs respond in two ways to certain stress factors: with redirected behaviour or with aggressive behaviour. Aggression can turn into biting/redirected behaviour, but not the other way round.

Picture puzzle
What does this behaviour tell you?

Piglet 3 and piglet 4 are fighting. Aggression is always directed to the front of the pig. Piglet 1 is displaying redirected behaviour. Piglet 2 is a passive responder. It tolerates the bullying from piglet 1 without doing anything. Piglet 2 has already been bitten once on the ear.

Redirected behaviour

Redirected behaviour results from exploratory behaviour, where the pig roots and begins to bite or chew on things. In the wild, it would chew on plant roots, grass or herbaceous plants. Play materials such as barrels and chains cannot satisfy these exploring and chewing tendencies, but straw can.

In a pen without suitable bedding, an exploring pig will bite the ears, tails, flanks or legs of other pigs. This is referred to as redirected behaviour. The animal wants to bite on something fibrous but nothing is available, so it directs its chewing urge towards another pig.

Straw also provides a satiated feeling, due to the full stomach and the digestive products of the crude fibre in the large intestine (volatile fatty acids).

Aggression

All pig behaviours have an aim, including fighting (aggression). First, pigs fight to establish a dominance hierarchy. Second, they fight for food. Third, they respond aggressively to ensure their peace and quiet.

Fights for dominance are decided in one day. After this the animals use subtle signals to confirm their dominance ranking, such as avoidance. But in order to give out and see such signals, they need sufficient space.

This pig wants to eat but cannot, so it bites the tail of the pig that is eating. Tail biting is a form of redirected behaviour, as are flank biting and leg biting. The biting of ear tips can also originate from redirected behaviour.

When displaying aggression, pigs butt each other with their heads, aiming at the front of their opponent: head, ears, neck, shoulders. In full pens, pigs will also attack other body parts. A head butt with an open mouth indicates a high level of aggression. The damage to this ear tip appears older than the fight wounds.

Reasons for redirected behaviour
● inadequate feed/feeling of hunger
● not being able to eat simultaneously, draughts and/or cold
● no peaceful resting area
● being sick or becoming sick and not being able to wallow
● discomfort and pain
● premature weaning
● not being able to wallow

Reasons for agression
● mixing unknown pigs, too little feed
● not being able to eat simultaneously
● draughts
● being sick or becoming sick
● improper pen layout (route from feeding area to defecation area crosses lying area)
● not being able to wallow

Prevention of redirected behaviour

As a pig acquires more control over its situation, it will display less undesired behaviour. This depends on the following:

- An available rest area with a good climate.
- The animals are sufficiently satiated.
- They do not have to fight for food.
- Aggression is minimal and avoidable.
- They can satisfy their exploratory urges with suitable chewing material.
- The pigs must be healthy.

A handful of straw per pig per day has a significant effect in preventing biting. The pig can satisfy its exploratory urge and feels satiated. Beet pulp also provides satiation and therefore peace and quiet. However, beet pulp results in sticky dung.

Fragile balance

In a pen where a pig has few options for solving problems and avoiding disturbances, the climate, housing, nutrition and care must be excellent. This is a fragile situation. A disturbance of the peace and quiet can quickly lead to problem behaviour, after which it is difficult to restore the balance.

Aggression
Pigs attack each other and fight.

Redirected behaviour
The pigs explore, biting and wanting to chew.

Agitation

Rest

Pigs set in → Time

Peace and quiet

If healthy pigs have sufficient space and rest areas and enough to eat, disturbances will cause only temporary agitation. There is almost always peace and quiet in the group. Aggression is rare (mixing). There is little biting behaviour.

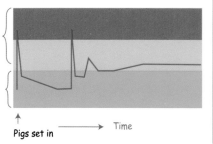

Aggression
Short-lived, avoidance behaviour is possible

Redirected behaviour
Exploratory urge satisfied with rooting and chewing material

Agitaion

Rest

→ Time

Intervene when pigs bite

Generally it is a single pig that begins to bite. Isolate the pig that was bitten as quickly as possible so that the wound can heal. Usually the animal can return after a week. At the same time, tackle the cause of the biting.

If the biting pig has tasted blood, it will not be easy to stop the animal from biting again. It will now bite to taste blood. The only solution is to separate the group and provide them with more space. Give the animals straw bedding and ensure that the wounds heal properly.

Biting behaviour with oozing wounds requires a rigorous approach. The pigs must heal and they must stop biting. Eliminate the cause so it doesn't happen again.

Look-think-act
What came first: ear necrosis or ear biting?

What came first: ear necrosis or ear biting?

Biting and sucking lead to injury of the ear tip, which in turn can lead to a bacterial infection. This is caused by bacteria on the skin (staphylococci), sometimes together with bacteria in the blood (streptococci).

Ear necrosis often occurs in combination with diseases, possibly because sick pigs display less avoidance behaviour or because sick pigs display redirected behaviour. Sickness may also affect the dominance hierarchy, which causes fighting.

And there is more. General diseases, such as streptococcal infections and PRRS/mycoplasma, can lead to a situation where the body concentrates the blood supply in the important organs. The result is poor blood circulation in the skin and extremities, such as the points of the ears and the tail. Reduced circulation makes it easier for infections to take hold. Numbness also occurs; as a result, the pig does not respond to being bitten. *Disease stimulates ear necrosis, but biting is the cause.*

Satiation

Food is a pig's primary motivation. The satiated feeling of a full stomach is the main pre-condition for peace and quiet. Hunger results in agitation.

Enough for everyone

Finishing pigs must be fed in such a way that every animal in the group can eat enough. If they are given continuous access to feed, the trough should not be empty when you refill it. With dosed feeding, all animals must have an eating place and every location must have the same amount of food. Gilts and boars can be fed unlimited amounts throughout the finishing process, but castrated males will become obese. This means that castrated males should get less feed than they want to eat. This is very important with continuous access feeding because then the dominant pigs gorge themselves and those with lower status eat little. Continuous access feeding is still possible if you provide a feed that is filling but not too high in energy content. It is feasible to feed pigs limited amounts in a dosage system with automated feed stations. The station recognises each pig and provides the correct portion.

These pigs are thin even though there is feed in the trough. This is a signal that they might not be drinking enough water.

Pigs spill a great deal of feed in a feed trough that is open too wide. Moreover, if they make a lot of wet feed, it is very probable that they will plug up the nipple drinker and the feed trough.

Automatic feed dispensers should release only five to ten pellets of feed with every eating motion, so there should be very little feed in the container. The pool of water shows that the nipple drinker is giving water (at least 1 l/min.).

These feed troughs are automatically filled and the pigs dive in to eat. This means that they are getting too little to eat. To see this you must periodically observe the pigs when the troughs are filled. And listen carefully, because pigs typically make high-pitched stress calls when fighting over food.

Warm-cold behaviour

Pigs cool themselves by their breathing and through their skin. They do not have any sweat glands. The first signal that the pen temperature is too high is rapid breathing. This occurs above 22°C. High humidity makes pigs more susceptible to heat.

The optimal temperature for a 60 kg pig is around 18°C. Above this, feed intake declines and the risk of pen soiling increases. Excessive warmth (heat stress) causes serious problems for a pig.

On the other hand, if it becomes too cold, the pigs eat more and they begin to crowd together and lie on each other . The lower limit of temperature is related to the air velocity near the pig. Every ventilation system has risk areas. Find these risk areas and check them. Also think about the pen near the entrance, near the fan or near an outside wall. At these locations the climate can be sub-optimal, even though it is good in the other pens.

These pigs are lying on their sides, just touching. They are also lying in the desired lying area. This is a signal that they feel comfortable: not too warm, not too cold, and there are no draughts.

Despite being disturbed by their neighbours, these piglets are lying on the slats and not on the more peaceful area with the solid floor. They also have their defecation area on the slats. Probably the solid floor is too warm.

Look-think-act
What does this lying behaviour tell you?

The pigs are not lying on the convex floor against the side wall, but on the slats. Slats are usually cooler than solid floors. The pigs have made their defecation area along the wall. It may have been too cold next to the wall, so when the pigs were set in they chose to make their lying place next to the feeding trough. Check the wall insulation (measure wall temperature).

Light · Feed · Water · Air · Peace & quiet · Space · Health

Sick pigs require early and effective treatment

Recognise risks as early as possible and respond as quickly as possible. This is essential when dealing with sick pigs. Actually you should respond in advance: anticipate the situation so that everything continues to go well. For example, you can implement feed changes gradually and change the ventilation before the nights get cold. But some problems cannot be foreseen, such as influenza. Other risks are always lurking as well, such as the intestinal infection PIA Andrtain risks simply require your full attention, such as the first few weeks after setting in.

Measuring body temperature

You measure the body temperature of pigs in the rectum via the anus. If a pig is sick, the temperature is high (fever), up to 42°C in some circumstances. A high ambient temperature, stress and exertion also increase body temperature. The temperature of healthy pigs tells you what is normal in the section or the group.

Categories	Body temperature
Piglet 1-8 weeks	39-40°C
Piglet 8-12 weeks	39-40°C
Finishing pig	39-40°C
Sows, boars	38-38.5°C

Points of attention for animal inspection

Signal	Early/late	Action
Doesn't get up quickly	Early	Caution
Stomach not full	Early	Look further
Agitation, redirected behaviour	Early	Look further
Rapid breathing	Fairly early	Look further
Belly not filled	Fairly early	Intervene
Doesn't come to eat	Fairly early	Intervene
Remains in one place	Fairly early	Intervene
Arched back	Fairly early	Intervene
Hair stands on end	Fairly early	Intervene
Pale, long hair	Fairly late	Intervene
Straggler	Late	Intervene
Low feed intake (kg)	Very late	Improve process
Slow growth	Very late	Improve process
Low uniformity	Very late	Improve process

A list of inspection points. Many livestock managers use points from this list without realising it. However, by deliberately recording your observations, you improve quality, you learn things and you can intervene more effectively.

Picture puzzle
What do you see? How did this happen?

Pig 1 is standing with an arched back and an empty stomach. Pig 2 and pig 3 have full stomachs. Determine why Pig 1 has an arched back and is not eating. Is it lame, is it sick or is there no feed or water available? You can observe lameness, you can determine sickness by measuring for fever and you can check on the feed and water.

Respond effectively

You treat a pig to promote its recovery and to ensure that the disease does not spread further.

Euthanasia or slaughter

Euthanasia or slaughtering are suitable solutions for pigs with poor prospects of recovery or improvement. Make timely decisions concerning euthanasia or culling. Discuss the decision criteria with an expert. Make sure you have excellent transport and professional euthanasia or slaughtering available.

Remove the cause

A bacterial or parasitic infection can be treated with anti-biotics or anti-parasitic agents to kill the pathogens or slow their growth. As yet there is no medication against viruses. The pig's immune system must deal with the existing infection. Treat the animal periodically to prevent opportunistic infections.

Injecting medication ensures that the pig has received the correct dosage. Sick pigs usually continue to drink, but eat less or not at all, so it is preferable to medicate the herd via the drinking water. Always follow the vet's instructions and read the directions that accompany the medication.

Controlling symptoms

Pain, swelling and the exudation of fluids are normal aspects of a disease process. However these symptoms do slow recovery and must therefore be alleviated as much as possible.

Sodium salicylate is an example of a pain reliever/anti-inflammatory drug (NSAID: non-steroid anti-inflammatory drug). Such drugs ensure better recovery of affected organs. In addition, the pig will be more active and will eat and drink more.

There are also other medications for symptom control.

Care

A pig cannot recover without good feed and water intake. The sick animal also needs rest and a comfortable resting place (sickbed).

Provide sick pigs with a constant supply of good and appetising food , along with clean, fresh water. Separate sick pigs immediately so you can make sure they can eat and drink (they will still be able to recognise their pen mates after five weeks of separation). Also provide an excellent lying area, with a comfortable and healthy climate. Sick pigs require a higher ambient temperature.

Quarantine

Sick animals excrete large numbers of pathogens. All their bodily fluids can transmit disease. Nose contact, coughing and sneezing exacerbate this process.

Quarantine the sick pigs, pens or sections. Do not walk or work from sick pigs to healthy pigs. Use separate sets of tools and materials. Initiate this protocol immediately and continue using it for at least three weeks after recovery.

CHAPTER 7

Handling and treating pigs

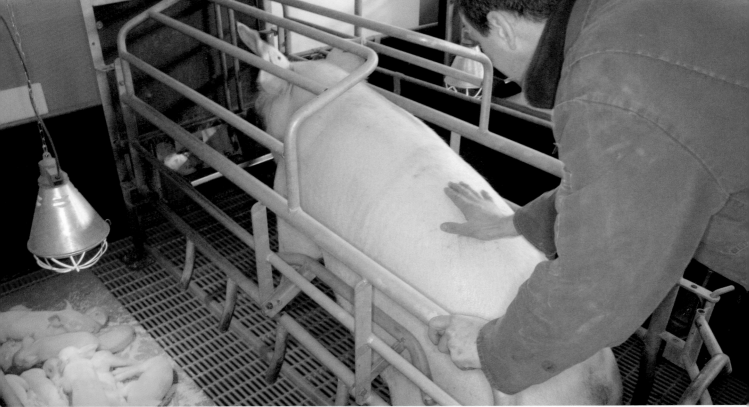

When you handle pigs, their unique characteristics become abundantly clear. Knowledge of pig characteristics helps to avoid unnecessary problems, stress and mistakes. Consider factors such as the pig dominance hierarchy, the way a pig navigates and its the natural responses to disturbances.

Touching and talking calmly to pigs leads to an outstanding people-pig relationship.

There is plenty of evidence that dealing with pigs in a calm and friendly fashion ensures peaceful surroundings and higher production. In addition, working calmly is essential to high quality work, and working with calm pigs is much more enjoyable than working with agitated, jittery animals. Frightened pigs are also much more difficult to drive to a different pen, a truck or the slaughterhouse.

This older sow is showing the gilt her place at the bottom of the hierarchy. The sow makes herself as big as possible and looks downward (dominant behaviour). The gilt makes herself as small as possible and avoids the sow (submissive behaviour).

Handling pigs

If you have to carry out a procedure on heavier pigs, it is best to drive them close together so that every pig is actually immobilised. If this is not sufficient a noose pole can offer a solution. Place a loop around the upper jaw, behind the canine teeth, with the knot on the bridge of the nose. The pig responds by pulling back, tightening the noose (and by screaming).

Points of attention for controlling animals with a noose pole:
- work as quickly as possible
- minimise pain and discomfort
- reward the animal afterwards (feed, straw, etc.)

Lifting small piglets

The best way to pick up a small piglet is to hold and lift it by its loin area.
Support the animal as quickly as possible with a second hand.

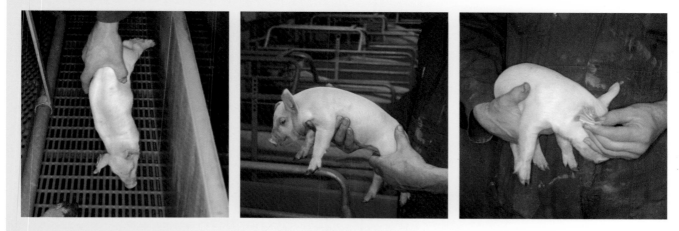

Lifting heavier piglets

Hold heavier piglets by a hind leg and lift them up with the other arm under the chest.
Lift heavy, well-muscled piglets by the groin fold and not by the hind leg.

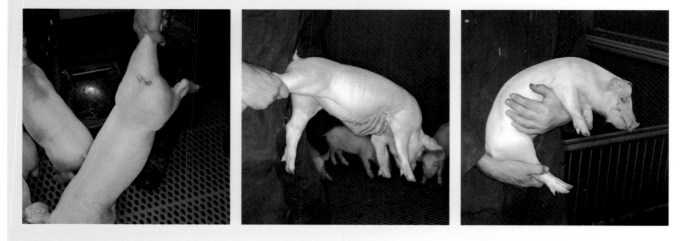

Looking around

Pigs like to root around for their food. They look for food close to the ground and prefer to move around in thick undergrowth. If they are afraid, they tend to run between or underneath things rather than over things.

While people navigate primarily with their eyes, scents and sounds are at least as important to a pig. Pigs do not see as well as people, especially long-distance. Moreover, their field of vision is much narrower.

The eyes of a pig are primarily adapted to searching for food. During this process the animal looks down along its nose.

Foto: Kees Scheepens

How a pig navigates

This sow is being driven out of the farrowing house. In the aisle, she lifts up her head to look around. While walking she will often defecate and urinate.

This is the normal way a pig explores its surroundings: with its head down to feel, smell and taste.

This is more or less what a sow sees when she walks through a straw-bedded pen with her head lifted fairly high. Hanging ears reduce her field of view even further.

Moving pigs

If you deliberately take advantage of the natural reactions of pigs, driving them from one location to another is not difficult. Besides the above points for attention, it is important to organise your work properly: prepare well, have enough help and try not to do two things at once. Whenever possible, move groups of pigs and not individuals. The animals are easy to move together. Give them time to sniff around. Don't allow them to become fearful of certain people or certain situations. Stay calm.

A uniform floor surface, straight walls and walking towards the light are several basic conditions for smooth pig transport.

Points for attention when moving pigs

- level floor, horizontal, even colour, no unusual objects
- no disturbing sounds
- have them walk from dark to light
- no moving objects, people, shadows or light
- no glare, no bright light
- no disturbing objects, fences or blind spots
- solid side walls.

Pig boards are an essential aid to keep pigs calm and to drive them efficiently.

If you slide a bucket over her head, the sow moves backwards because she wants to get her head out of the bucket.

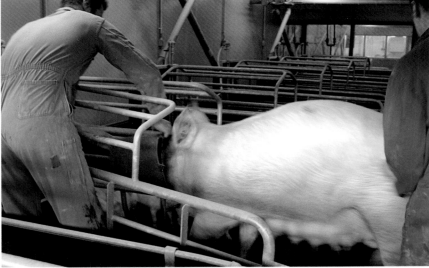

Standard Working Method

For every action, a Standard Working Method (SWM) can be formulated. By always working in the same way, you prevent errors and you can more easily improve the procedure. A Standard Working Method has the following structure: preparation, the procedure itself, monitoring during the work and checking the results.

Standard Working Method example 1: tail docking

Tails are docked due to the risk of biting by other pigs. The procedure is painful and stressful for the piglet. Recovery requires energy and the wound poses an infection risk, so dock tails very carefully. If tail biting occurs, look for the underlying cause. After all, docking does not prevent biting, but only reduces the temptation to bite.

Preparation

1 Organise a work area with plenty of light and sufficient space. Make sure you can work calmly and in a controlled fashion, with all tools within reach.

2 Check to make sure the burner is sufficiently hot and there are no burrs on it.

The work itself

3 Immobilise the litter, so that you can pick up the piglets quickly and easily.

4 Place the tail on the work surface; cut from the underside of the tail to the upper side.

5 Dock the tail to 1.5 cm in length using a red-hot burner.

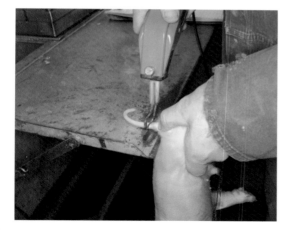

6 Allow the burner to drop slowly through the tail so that the wound is properly cauterised.

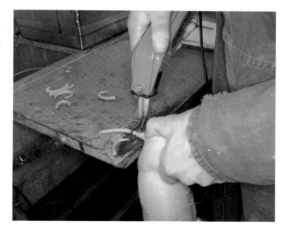

7 Return the piglet to a quiet place.
ENSURE THAT THE PIGLET NEST IS IN PERFECT ORDER. Recovering piglets need warmer surroundings.

Monitoring during the work

8 The stump is completely cauterised and does not bleed.

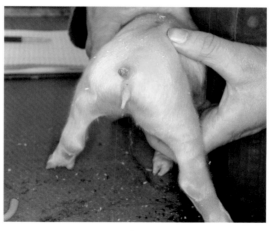

9 Ten minutes after docking: no blood can be seen on more than 90% of the piglets.

Checking the results

10 Three days after docking, more than 90% of the wounds are dry, not swollen and have no red edges.

Standard Working Method example 2: Intra-muscular injections

Injecting pigs is a standard procedure on all farms. Follow the steps below for a correct working method for intra-muscular injections (i.m.), and always read the label thoroughly beforehand.

Preparation

1 Organise a good working area. Place needles, injection fluids and syringe within reach, ensure that there is sufficient light, a clean working surface if necessary, etc.

2 Take a new needle of the correct length and diameter.

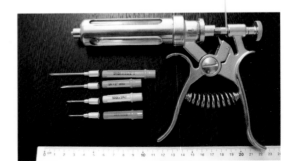

3 Use an injection fluid that is guaranteed to be clean and effective. If in doubt, do not use it.

4 Puncture the bottle with a clean needle. Even better, use an automatic syringe system.

The work itself

5 Inject at the correct site.

Piglet

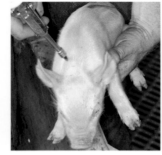

The correct injection site is just in front of the shoulder blade above the neck vertebrae, in the muscle.

Now and again, inject piglets under the supervision of a vet, who can tell if you are doing it properly.

Older pig

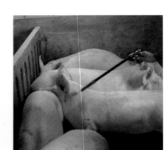

The correct injection site is just in front of the shoulder blade above the neck vertebrae, in the neck muscle.

6 Ensure that the pig is standing still. An injection needle inside a moving neck can do a lot of damage!

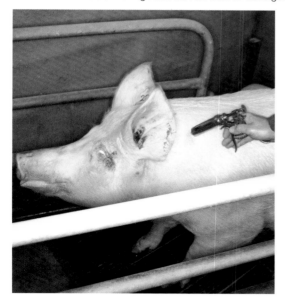

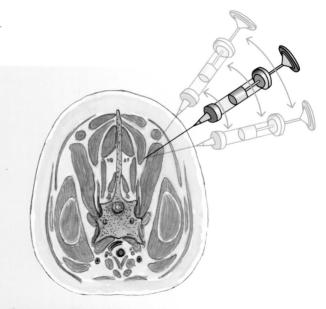

Cross section of the neck
The injection fluid ends up between the neck muscles. If you inject incorrectly you can hit bones, blood vessels, tendons and nerves. Any pathogens on the needle or in the fluid can be easily transmitted.

7 Mark the injected pigs; use codes, such as a different colour for every day.

8 Replace disposable needles regularly, for example, after every litter.

Completing the procedure

9 Never inject fluid back into the bottle!

10 Dispose of used needles safely.

11 Clean the syringe.

12 Place the injection fluid in the refrigerator. Caution: some injection fluids should not be refrigerated. This information is on the label.

13 How do you monitor the quality of this work?

Standard Working Method example 3: castration using anaesthetic

A local anaesthetic reduces pain during and after castration. Consequently, the castration proceeds more easily and you can work more carefully. Moreover, the piglet will continue to eat better and will heal more quickly.

Use a clean, very sharp knife. Make sure your hands are clean. Disinfect both before and after castrating.

The work itself

1 Inject the local anaesthetic into both testicles and under the skin at the site of the incision.

2 Make a single incision through the skin. Do not cut the testicles. The incision is fairly low, so that any fluid can easily escape.

3 Push the testicle outside through the incision.

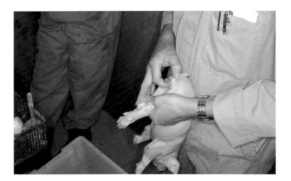

4 Remove the testicle, together with the spermatic cord, in a single motion.

5 Inspect the wound carefully: are you sure that nothing is sticking out?

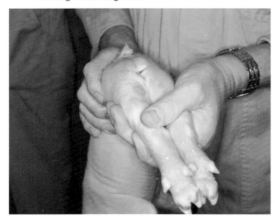

Post-inspection

6 The wound on the right is healing well. However, the cord in the wound on the left is preventing it from closing and allowing bacteria to enter.

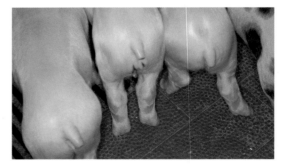

Index

PIG SIGNALS

The book **Pig Signals** is part of an extensive programme to improve the knowledge of pig farmers.

Group **presentations** and **study club evenings** are based on photographs, images and sounds from the daily practice of pig farmers. Questions are answered in an unconventional fashion and the audience becomes actively involved in the presentation.

On-farm training sessions are also provided during which the participants encounter behavioural signals in the pens that they may not have noticed with their own pigs. These on-farm sessions are always surprising.

The aim of the activities is to

- prevent 'farm blindness'
- include evaluations as part of your daily routine
- brush up your practical knowledge
- learn to work with checklists
- improve the performance of your pig herd

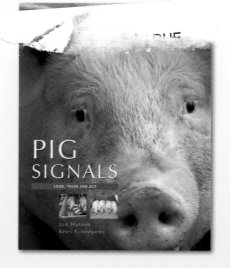

...nore information, please contact:

PUBLISHERS

P.O. Box 4103
NL-7200 BC Zutphen
Telephone: +31 575 54 56 88
Fax: +31 575 54 69 90
E-mail: info@roodbont.nl
Internet: www.roodbont.nl

VETVICE
Making veterinary knowledge work

Moerstraatsebaan 115
NL-4614 PC Bergen op Zoom
Telefoon: : +31 165 30 43 05
Fax: +31 165 30 37 58
E-mail: info@vetvice.nl
Internet: www.vetvice.nl

Food Safety
Animal Health
Animal Welfare

DR. C.J.M. SCHEEPENS CONSULTANCY B.V

Hogevleutweg 5
NL-5681 PD Best
Telephone/Fax: +31 499 31 01 42
E-mail: kscheepens@aol.com
Internet: www.3drie3.nl

AGRICULTURAL PUBLICATIONS FROM ROODBONT

In addition to Pig Signals, Roodbont offers many other practical books about various aspects of agriculture. You can order these publications directly from our website (www.roodbont.nl), by telephone (+31 575 54 56 88) or by e-mail (info@roodbont.nl). For orders from abroad, we charge for shipping (the minimum shipping cost is € 5.00).

ISBN 90-75280-65-3

96 pages, price € 25.90 (£ 17.90)

COW SIGNALS
A practical guide for dairy farm management

Cows send out signals continuously about their health, well-being, nutrition and production. The challenge for the dairy farmer is how to interpret and use these signals. Dutch vet and cow enthusiast Jan Hulsen has drawn on his expertise and extensive experience with cows and dairy farmers to write Cow Signals: a richly-illustrated farmer's guide on how to interpret the behaviour, posture and physical characteristics of groups of cows and individual animals.

'Cows send out useful information every moment of the day. Are you receiving it?'

When observing cows it is important not to jump to conclusions immediately, but instead to always ask yourself three questions:

- What do I see?
- Why has this happened?
- What does this mean?

For example, a lump on a cow's shoulder could indicate that something is wrong with the feed barrier, and if cows remain standing in their cubicles, this is a sign of poor cubicle comfort. Armed with such information, you can take appropriate remedial action. If you know what to look for, you can pick up the signals everywhere and anytime. Cow Signals will show you how.